"This volume is the encapsula
teaching by one of the most bi
Herein, Turco has admirably compiled and expanded the most
critical information any student of chant should assimilate. The text
begins with an overview of the history of chant, which is both concise
and informative, adding details that are not commonly known. The
heart of the work focuses on chant: first, on its text; second, on the
melody; and ultimately, on the union of text and melody, which is
fundamentally different from setting texts to melodies. Turco reminds
us that understanding chant must start with understanding its text.
This is a welcome addition to the pedagogical materials on the
subject, for the study of chant melodies and especially chant rhythms,
along with the ancient rhythmic signs, can only be successful if it is
grounded on an understanding of the text and its particular nuances.
Turco's approach to the text, and ultimately to the wedding of text and
melody, is thorough and masterful. It renders this volume an essential
addition to the library of any student or teacher of chant."

— Edward Schaefer, President, The Collegium

"We are fortunate to have this excellent translation of Alberto Turco's
The Gregorian Melody: The Expressive Power of the Word by Stephen
Concordia, OSB. It is the first time that we have realized the true
relationship between the neumes and the words they express.
I recommend this book most highly."

— Ann Labounsky, Chair of Organ and Sacred Music,
   Duquesne University

The Gregorian Melody

The Expressive Power of the Word

Alberto Turco

Translated by Stephen Concordia, OSB

LITURGICAL PRESS
Collegeville, Minnesota

www.litpress.org

About the cover: Art by Ruberval Monteiro da Silva, OSB.
The image is the "Merkabah" or "God's chariot of fire." From Ezekiel's visions, the Lord used a "wheel" to reveal his presence not only in Jerusalem's temple but where his people were held in exile. In the Christian interpretation, the Son of God is the real Presence among us, and in the book of Revelation, this symbolic image confirms it. The power of the living Word of Christ was also seen by identification with the four gospels written about Jesus.

Originally published as Antiquæ Monodiæ Eruditio – I, *La melodia gregoriana: forza espressiva della Parola* (Roma: Edizioni Torre d'Orfeo, 2004)

© 2023 by Stephen Concordia, OSB
Published by Liturgical Press, Collegeville, Minnesota. All rights reserved. No part of this book may be used or reproduced in any manner whatsoever, except brief quotations in reviews, without written permission of Liturgical Press, Saint John's Abbey, PO Box 7500, Collegeville, MN 56321-7500. Printed in the United States of America.

1	2	3	4	5	6	7	8	9

Library of Congress Cataloging-in-Publication Data

Names: Turco, Alberto, author. | Concordia, Stephen, OSB, translator.
Title: The Gregorian melody : the expressive power of the word / Alberto Turco ; translated by Stephen Concordia, OSB.
Other titles: Melodia gregoriana. English
Description: Collegeville, Minnesota : Liturgical Press, 2023. | Summary: "A resource of music pedagogy, The Gregorian Melody includes insights into the Gregorian art and proposes that chant is first and foremost sung prayer, an interaction of word and melody, which both include proper and appropriate expression. The material included in this resource is foundational as it lays out the elements of the Gregorian melody through a careful analysis of first principles. It will be useful as an introduction to Gregorian chant and for helping readers to understand the Gregorian melody. Readers of all levels may turn to this book to sing the liturgical chant with a deepened appreciation for the expressive power of the Word"— Provided by publisher.
Identifiers: LCCN 2023006606 (print) | LCCN 2023006607 (ebook) | ISBN 9780814667675 (paperback) | ISBN 9780814667682 (epub) | ISBN 9780814667682 (pdf) | ISBN 9798400800283 (pdf)
Subjects: LCSH: Gregorian chants—History and criticism. | Gregorian chants—Analysis, appreciation.
Classification: LCC ML3082 .T92 2023 (print) | LCC ML3082 (ebook) | DDC 782.32/22—dc23/eng/20230215
LC record available at https://lccn.loc.gov/2023006606
LC ebook record available at https://lccn.loc.gov/2023006607

Confitemini Domino
In cithara
in psalterio decem cordarum
psallite ei
canticum novum.
(Ps 32:2, 3)

Sing him a new song.
Strip off your oldness,
you know a new song.
A new person,
a New Covenant,
a new song.
People stuck in the old life
have no business
with this new song;
only they can learn it
who are new persons,
renewed by grace
and throwing off the old,
sharers already in the New Covenant,
which is the kingdom of heaven.
All our love yearns toward that,
and in its longing
our love sings a new song.
Let us sing this new song
not with our tongues
but with our lives.

Sing him a new song,
sing skillfully to him.
Each one of us is anxious
to know how to sing to God.
Sing to him, yes,
but not out of tune.
We don't want to grate on his ears.
Sing skillfully to him, my friend.
Do not worry,
for he provides you
with a technique for singing.
Do not go seeking lyrics,
as though you could spell out in words
anything that will give God pleasure.
Sing to him *in jubilation.*

(Exposition 2 of Psalm 32, from St. Augustine, *Expositions of the Psalms*, part III, vol. 15, trans. Maria Boulding, OSB [Hyde Park, NY: New City Press, 2000]. Used with permission.)

CONTENTS

ABBREVIATIONS

Cited sources

ALB   cod. Paris, Bibl. Nat. lat. 776, *Graduale-tropario,* second half of eleventh century (CG 3)

AM   *Antiphonale Monasticum*, Paris, Tournai, Rome, 1934

AMM   *Antiphonale Missarum, iuxta ritum Sanctæ Ecclesiæ Mediolanensis*, Rome, 1935

AR   *Antiphonale Sacrosanctae Romanae Ecclesiæ pro diurnis horis*, Paris, Tournai, Rome, 1924

AS   *Antiphonale Missarum Simplex iuxta ritum Sanctæ Ecclesiæ Mediolanensis*, Milan, 2001

CG   *Codices Gregoriani*, eds. N. Albarosa, H. Rumphorst and A. Turco, Padova, 3 vols. (1991–2001)

GL   H. Keil, *Grammatici Latini*, 7 vols., Leipzig, Teubner, 1856–1880

GR   *Graduale Sacrosanctæ Romanæ Ecclesiæ*, Solesmes, 1974

GREG   Gregorian repertory

GS   *Graduale Simplex, editio typica altera*, Typis Polyglottis Vaticanis, 1975

GT   *Graduale Triplex*, ed. M.-C. Billecocq and R. Fischer, Solesmes, 1979

HISP   Spanish or Mozarabic repertory

KR   *Kyriale Romanum,* Solesmes, 1985

LH	*Liber hymnarius, cum Invitatoriis & aliquibus Responsoriis*, "Antiphonale Romanum, secundum Liturgiam Horarum" Tomus alter, Solesmes, 1983
Lon	cod. London, British Museum, add. 34209, twelfth century (PM I, 5-6)
LR	*Liber responsorialis*, Solesmes, 1895
LU	*Liber Usualis Missa: et Officii pro Dominicis et Festis*, Tournai–Rome–New York, 1960
MA	*Missale Ambrosianum, iuxta ritum Sanctæ Mediolanensis*, Milan, 1981
MD	*Graduale Medicea: De Tempore*, 1614 (Anastatic reproduction, Vatican City, 2001)
MIL	Ambrosian chant repertory
MPG	*Monumenta Paleographica Gregoriana*, ed. G. Joppich, Münsterschwarzach, 4 vols.
MS	*Musicam Sacram*, Post Conciliar Instruction on Music in the Liturgy, Sacred Congregation of Rites, 1967
ND	*In Nocte Nativitatis Domini, ad Matutinum, Missam juxta ritum monasticum*, Paris, Tournai, Rome, 1936
OF	*Offertoriale sive Versus offertoriorum Cantus Gregoriani*, C. Ott, Paris, Tournai, Rome, 1935
PL	*Patrologia: cursus completus, Series latina*, ed. J.P. Migne, Paris-Montrouge, 1844–1864, 221 vols.
PM	Paléographie musicale, les principaux manuscrits de chant grégorien, ambrosien, mozarabe, gallican, First Series 1–22; Second Series 1–2, from 1899, Solesmes, Tournai, Bern
PsM	*Psalterium Monasticum*, Solesmes, 1981
RB	*Rule of St. Benedict 1980*, ed. Timothy Fry (Collegeville, MN: Liturgical Press, 1981)
SC	*Sacrosanctum Concilium*, Constitution on the Sacred Liturgy of the Second Vatican Council, 1963

SE   *Scriptores ecclesiastici de musica sacra potissimum*, ed. M. Gerbert, vol. I, Milan, 1931

VAT   Editio typica Vaticana

Chants

Ant.   Antiphon

Cant.   Canticum

Co.   *Antiphona ad communione*

Gr.   *Responsorium-graduale*

In.   *Antiphona ad introitum*

Of.   *Offertorium*

Tr.   *Tractus*

FOREWORD

The subtitle of this book announces the message that runs all through it: the Gregorian melody is not an aesthetic end in itself, but exists completely and entirely as the expressive power of the Word. In a sense, the melody is not *music* as we generally understand that term. It is, more fundamentally, *word* that comes to be expressed in a particular way by being sung.

With this understanding of the Gregorian melody, Msgr. Alberto Turco is firmly planted in the school of chant interpretation known as "semiology." Building upon the pioneering work of Eugène Cardine (1905–1988), monk of Solesmes Abbey, scholars have decoded the rhythmic meanings of the earliest lineless notation. It has become increasingly clear that subtleties of rhythmic nuance indicated in the lineless notation are rooted in the text. The manner of rendering the text ensures its careful and effective declamation, but even more, it presents a theological and spiritual interpretation of the text.

Turco rightly understands all of this within a liturgical context, for the texts of Gregorian chant are fundamentally ritual elements of the liturgy. The theological and spiritual message of the chant is the theological and spiritual message of the liturgy itself. It is especially significant that Turco writes from the standpoint of the Catholic liturgy as reformed by the Second Vatican Council (1962–1965). His work is intended to be of assistance in the prudent promotion of Gregorian chant in the liturgy as currently celebrated by the Catholic Church. (It goes without saying that this does not preclude the fruitful use of Latin chant in other contexts such as sacred concerts.)

Turco repeatedly emphasizes that this book is not about study for its own sake, but is ordered toward a living performance with a sense for text and liturgy. The book is the fruit of the work Turco himself has done for over forty years as conductor of the Nova Schola Gregoriana. This ensemble has won international critical acclaim and is renowned with awards for its singing. Turco is very much a scholar-practitioner. It could not be otherwise. It is years of singing Gregorian chant that occasioned reflection, gave rise to questions, aroused curiosity, and stimulated intensive investigation.

Turco brings to the field of chant scholarship a particular focus on the historical evolution of modality in the earliest centuries of chant before there was notation. While this work is necessarily speculative and hypothetical, with a certain amount of creative guesswork, the picture that Turco paints makes it abundantly clear that the modal development of melodies was driven at every turn by the inherent power of the word and the desire to express the word more effectively. Turco's reconstruction of how and when the melodies might have evolved is helpfully reinforced with knowledge of how the liturgy evolved in its ritual structures at various historical points.

One needs a firm understanding of the basics of music theory to follow the material in this book. The material is quite technical and analytical. In a sense the material is foundational, for it lays out the most basic elements of the Gregorian melody through a careful analysis of first principles. But these are the sort of first principles that one arrives at only after many years of study coupled with extensive experience of singing the Gregorian melodies. That is to say that the material in this book will be helpful at the outset as an introduction to Gregorian chant, but the material will come to take on more meaning when one returns to it after years and decades of experience with the Gregorian melodies. The reader will want to turn to this book as a beginner, as a more advanced practitioner, and as a seasoned veteran.

We all benefit from the careful and accurate English translation done by Fr. Stephen Concordia, OSB, of St. Vincent Archabbey. His labors make this important book available to a much wider readership.

May this book help the reader understand the Gregorian melody intellectually—and even more so, to sing the liturgical chant with a deepened appreciation for the expressive power of the Word.

Anthony Ruff, OSB
Saint John's Abbey, Advent 2021

AUTHOR'S PREFACE

Glancing at the table of contents of this volume, the reader is likely to be surprised not to find a chapter with specific references to neumes as would normally happen in a Gregorian chant manual. This volume focuses almost exclusively on the Latin text, on its style, and on the Latin accentuation that is the rhythmic-expressive source of the text and of the melody. These are the topics synthesized in the title *The Gregorian Melody: The Expressive Power of the Word.*

The Gregorian melody is the fruit of a compositional art generated by the syllables and words of the Latin text and matured through the mystical experience of a daily performance practice. It speaks in a language that exceeds the native prestige of its origins; and its expressive power, drawn from the eternal Word, is able to communicate with every culturally and spiritually prepared person.

The neumatic notation of the tenth century marks the passage from the oral transmission of the Gregorian melody to the written one. Even with the poverty of signs (*neumes*) it possesses, it is remarkably able to graphically translate the qualities of the sounds: in relation to the literary texts, to the aesthetic-modal forms of the melody, and to the phonetic aspects of the syllabic articulations and punctuation of the melodic-verbal phrasing. This is all the Gregorian composers needed to know. They did not ask the neumatic notation to provide an exact intervallic position of the notes, and not even the rhythmic indications of the verbal style within the melody, because the oral tradition was there, and because the knowledge of Latin was completely familiar.

The Gregorian composers spoke Latin: they knew the meaning of the words and their grammatical, logical and stylistic functions.

Above all they knew the rhythm of the text, its rhythmic unity, and, in the succession of these, its rhythmic equilibrium. For them, verbal style constitutes the foundational layer of the musical composition.

Today, this knowledge and practice of the Latin language, essential presuppositions for a correct interpretation and performance of Gregorian chant, are not at all familiar. They are no longer part of our culture. The necessity to fill in this gap, at least in part, as an initiation into the study of chant before undertaking the specific study of the paleographic Gregorian notation, is obvious. Significant and wise, in this regard, is the testimony of one of the most famous authorities on Gregorian composition, the former choirmaster of the renowned Abbey of Solesmes, Dom Jean Claire:

> Semiology is at the service of the text. If the word, if the phrase, do not flow from the process of *accentuation*—which has nothing to do with romanticism but, rather, is a requirement of an "existential" logic—every semiological detail added to this absence of linear direction, even if it is true, real, and objective, will inevitably bear false results and will not come to a suitable expression. Even to call upon the splendid voices of professional singers is useless: if they do not possess the fundamental "verbal style," their beautiful voices will not sing "Gregorian style" (*gregoriano modo*). It is even more difficult for them to assimilate the verbal style than the details of semiology: neumatic break, the values of the notes and their repercussions. Contemporary music demands many more difficult things from them, but still does not at all prepare them to sing a word or a phrase in a natural way, nor to give just the right amount, unaffectedly, with ease, and for the living synthesis of the two, maintaining in every moment one eye on the word and one on the phrase.[1]

In conclusion, the reader should not forget two very important points:

---

1. Cf. J. Claire, "Dom Eugène Cardine," *Études Grégoriennes* 23 (1989): 22.

1. Whatever help is offered by books or methods can never substitute for the living instruction of a trained master's concrete examples. This is even more true with a practical discipline such as chant.

2. The Gregorian melody can be learned and assimilated only through assiduous practice.

Note:

In the chants from the GR transcribed in this volume, some melodic variants have been introduced. This is a proposal for a melodic restitution—obviously of a private nature, for the purposes of study and which does not intend to interfere with the *typica* edition of the VAT—limited to the variants that the most reliable manuscript sources confirm in the light of the data acquired from the sciences of paleography and Gregorian semiology.

Furthermore, the use of rhythmic signs (dot, vertical and horizontal episema) are used to indicate punctuation of phrasing and rhythmic articulations of the melodic-verbal units. As regards, in particular, the horizontal episema, it is further used to complete those neumes to which the manuscript sources have applied it. Finally, the quarter barline is brought into the literary text whenever it is not possible to insert it in the musical staff.

INTRODUCTION

1. Gregorian chant: sung prayer

In common discourse on Gregorian chant there are still many who would define it as *cantus planus*, (a term used to indicate a melody in a lower register, distinct from *cantus acutus)* or as *cantus firmus*—or *cantus immesuratus* (in Italian *canto fermo*; in French *plain-chant*; in English *plainchant*; in German *Choral*—that is, rhythmically "free," different from music expressed in notes of "proportional duration" in time),[1] or as a collection of monophonic melodies with which are sung the texts of the liturgy of the Roman Church. Therefore, if one were to simply pick up a book of Gregorian chant, one might get an imprecise idea of it, namely, that of a musical "score" of pieces whose melodies are drawn in more or less long successions of square notes.

The exact definition of Gregorian, certainly to be extended to the other ancient repertories of the West such as the Ambrosian, for instance, is: *monody of the ritual Word*. Gregorian is, above all, a monody inseparably tied to texts; specifically, to Latin prose texts, drawn, for the most part, from the Bible, in particular from the Book of Psalms. It is a *chant*, therefore, and not music, nor pure melody;[2] it is a "ritual chant," the chant "proper" to the liturgy of

---

1. The definition of *cantus firmus* and *cantus planus*, as attributed to Gregorian chant, comes from the twelfth and thirteenth centuries, at the beginnings of the first polyphonic forms (*discantus*), in which the notes of a Gregorian melody provided a support of the various species of counterpoint, often in very long note values.

2. "Take away the word, the meaning, and what is the voice? Where there is no understanding, there is only a meaningless sound. The voice without the

the Roman Church, whose primary quality is "prayer," whether announcing the Word of God in the proclamation of the readings, or in the thanksgiving of the solemn eucharistic prayer, or when it becomes the praying voice of a community asking for dialogue with God and wanting to manifest to him due submission of gratitude, and implore his blessing.

The following are some examples of solemn, sometimes dramatic, prayers of supplication:

1. *Ad te levavi*: Introit antiphon of the First Sunday of Advent (p. 191 ex. A.1).
To you, I lift up my soul, O my God.
In you I have trusted; let me not be put to shame.
Nor let my enemies exult over me;
And let none who hope in you be put to shame. (Ps 25[24]:1-3)
Ad te levavi animam meam, Deus meus, in te confido, non erubescam neque irrideant me inimici mei. Et enim universi qui te expectant non confundentur.

2. *Circumdederunt me*: Introit antiphon of the ancient Lenten Mass of Lazarus (p. 192 ex. A.2).
The waves of death rose about me;
the pains of the netherworld surrounded me.
In my anguish I called to the Lord;
and from his holy temple he heard my voice. (Ps 18[17]:5, 7).
Circumdederunt me gemitus mortis, dolores inferni circumdederunt me: et in tribulatione mea invocavi Dominum, et exaudivit de templo sancto suo vocem meam.

3. *Miserere mihi*: Gradual, Wednesday, 3rd Week of Lent (p. 192 ex. A.3).
Have mercy on me, O Lord, for I am languishing;
O Lord, heal me. (Ps 6:2)

---

word strikes the ear but does not build up the heart" (St. Augustine, Discourse 293, 3; PL 1328–1329).

Vs. My bones are troubled. My soul also is sorely troubled.
(Ps 6:3-4).
Miserere mihi Domine, quoniam infirmus sum; sana me Domine.
Vs. Conturbata sunt omnia ossa mea: et anima mea turbata est valde.

These next texts announce a mystery, a divine blessing, and a Gospel fact, in inexplicable, joyous and robust chants:

4. *Resurrexi*: Introit Antiphon of Easter Sunday (p. 193 ex. A.4).
I have risen, and I am with you still, alleluia.
You have laid your hand upon me, alleluia.
Too wonderful for me, this knowledge, alleluia, alleluia.
(Ps 139[138]:18, 5-6)
Resurrexi et adhuc tecum sum, alleluia: posuisti super me manum tuam, alleluia:
mirabilis facta est scientia tua, alleluia.

5. *Cibavit eos*: Introit Antiphon for the Feast of Corpus Christi (p. 193 ex. A.5).
He fed them with the finest wheat
and satisfied them with honey from the rock. (Ps 81[80]:17)
Cibavit eos ex adipe frumenti, alleluia: et de petra, melle saturavit eos, alleluia.

6. *Factus est repente*: Communion Antiphon for the Solemnity of Pentecost; Gradual (p. 194 ex. A.6).
Suddenly there came a sound from heaven, the rushing of a mighty wind, coming from where they were sitting, alleluia.
They were all filled with the Holy Spirit and spoke of the marvels of God, alleluia. (Cf. Acts 2:2-4)
Factus est repente de caelo sonus, advenientis spiritus vehementis, ubi erant sedentes, alleluia: et replete sunt omnes Spiritu Sancto, loquentes magnalia Dei, alleluia.

These are only some of the many themes that Gregorian chant uses in order to fulfill the double purpose of the liturgy: the practice of the "complete and definitive public worship [of God]" and the "sanctification of women and men" (SC 7). Gregorian chant becomes in this way a sign, a gesture, and an expression of a sacred event. Beyond these considerations, one can never lose sight of the subjective aspect that must be present in every prayer: the *interior disposition*. Gregorian chant, though it possesses elements that are objectively good (words and melodies), nonetheless needs a soul for its interpretation; it needs a soul that prays, and that prays in song. This is the fundamental premise for an approach to the interpretation of these melodies. Assimilation of the text, and formation in appropriate ways of praying, are requisite steps along the way, so as to not fall into romantic "devotionalism" nor into formulations that are cold, empirical, or worse, arbitrary.[3]

2. Historical overview of Gregorian chant

The ancient roots of Western Christian chant reach as far back as the liturgical gatherings of the earliest Christian communities. From these it gradually evolved and spread by means of an oral tradition in which the melodies were sung without the help of any musical notation. The creation and subsequent elaboration of these melodies was strictly tied to the formation of the liturgical year and to the evolution and transformation of the musical forms,

---

3. In the Apostolic Letter *Orientale Lumen* (10) of May 2, 1995, Pope St. John Paul II wrote:

The starting point for the monk is the Word of God, a Word who calls, who invites, who personally summons, as happened to the Apostles. When a person is touched by the Word obedience is born, that is, the listening which changes life. Every day the monk is nourished by the bread of the Word. Deprived of it, he is as though dead and has nothing left to communicate to his brothers and sisters because the Word is Christ, to whom the monk is called to be conformed.

Even while he chants with his brothers the prayer that sanctifies time, he continues his assimilation of the Word. The very rich liturgical hymnody, of which all the Churches of the Christian East can be justly proud, is but the continuation of the Word which is read, understood, assimilated and finally sung: those hymns are largely sublime paraphrases of the biblical text, filtered and personalized through the individual's experience and that of the community.

the latter, with the introduction of the *schola* in the fifth and sixth centuries. It all came about in the course of eight centuries, during which texts and melodies grew in number and, as noted, were passed down by oral tradition. The various stages of composition are reflected in a multiplicity and heterogeneity of musical forms of different melodic genres, including (1) melody-types (melodies attached to multiple texts that are identified with, or at least are very close to, the archetype of a mode, p. 194 ex. A.7), (2) modal templates (melodies with multiple texts, that represent a development of the melody-type, p. 195 ex. A.8), (3) centonized melodies[4] (p. 196 ex. A.9), and (4) original melodies[5] (p. 197 ex. A.10).

There were two distinct periods of composition: that of the chants of the *psalmist*, and that of the *schola*. The first of these was characterized by the chants associated with the readings—*Graduale*, *Tractus* and *Canticum*—and were to be sung by the psalmist, at first in the form known as *in directum*, and later, in responsorial form. In this period, which lasted until the last quarter of the fifth century, there was no distinction between the liturgy of the Office and the liturgy of the Eucharist. In addition to the chants for the readings, in the Mass, there was the chant of Psalm 33—*Benedicam Dominum in omni tempore* (I will bless the Lord at all times)—to accompany the communion procession. This, in its responsorial form, has an Alleluia refrain during Easter season, and the refrain *Gustate et videte* when sung outside of the Easter season. Already at the time of St. Augustine (fourth century) there was, almost certainly, the chanting of a psalm for the presentation of the offerings.[6]

---

4. *Centonized* melodies (from the Latin *cento*, "a blanket or garment sewn with a worn woolen material") are created with formulas belonging to different modal idioms wisely sewn together by the composer to obtain a homogeneous and well-ordered whole.

5. An *original* melody is one born from the direct interpretation of the text, with its own ornamentation and without formulas from other modes.

6. St. Augustine, against the conservatives, defends the innovation of chanting the psalm *ante oblationem*:

A certain Hilary, a Catholic layman who had the title of Tribune, I don't know why, but following a somewhat widespread custom, once became greatly

With the organization of the liturgical prayer known as the Office (*Officium*), which consisted of the daily or weekly recitation of the entire Psalter so as to accomplish a "continual" prayer ("Pray without ceasing," 1 Thess 5:17), a new form of chanting the psalms with the alternation of two choirs was introduced in monastic and presbyteral communities.[7]

The second period, beginning from the last quarter of the fifth century, was characterized by the compositions of the chants for the schola: the processional chants (*Introit* and *Communio*) and the Alleluia in the Mass, and the chants of the Prolix, or Great, Responsories in the Office. The preexisting chants of the readings, and the Offertories, were re-composed at this time in a melodically ornate genre to accommodate the schola. The chants of the schola became a refined and learned repertory, sharply distinct from those of the psalmist's congregational or choral character.

The above liturgical, historical, and musical observations can be applied as well to the various regional traditions. Alongside the ancient repertory of the Church of Rome are found the Gallican (France), Mozarabic (Spain), Ambrosian (Milan), ancient Beneventan (central southern Italy), and Celtic (Ireland) repertories.

Gregorian chant, in the exact meaning of this term, has its origins in France in the eighth century, during the so-called Caro-

---

irritated with the ministers of God. Wherever he could, he attacked with malevolent criticisms the practice that had become popular in Carthage to intone hymns, taken from the Psalms, in front of the altar both before the offering as well as at the time that the offerings were distributed to the people—saying that this was something that should not be done.

7. The performance in alternation of two choirs includes chanting the psalms in the two great forms and second, that with a refrain, called *responsorialis*. In psalmody without a refrain the two choirs alternate in the singing of the verses of the psalm; in the psalmody with a refrain the two choirs alternate in the singing of both the verses of the psalm and of the refrain. It cannot be ruled out that, right from the beginning, the refrain would have been sung by the two choirs together. It would certainly be so when the refrain was to be sung only at the beginning and the end of the psalm.

lingian Renaissance. In the year 754, Pope Stephen II made an extraordinary visit to Gaul, to ask for political protection from Pepin, the King of the Franks. During the pope's stay at the Abbey of St. Denis, which concluded in October of 756, the idea emerged of a religious alliance with the Frankish Kingdom, which was to include the introduction of the liturgy of the Church of Rome into the regions of Gaul. Admiration for the Roman Rite, and the chant of the Papal Schola certainly provided significant motivation to implement such a historic event as was the reform of the Gallican liturgy. Among the promoters and architects of this reform were Pepin and his son Charlemagne. More importantly, however, were the bishop St. Chrodegang of Metz, the English monk Alcuin of York, and the bishop Amalarius, the most authoritative liturgist of the century, the last two both serving at the court of Charlemagne. Two master cantors of the Roman Schola also played significant roles: Peter, at the school of Metz, and Romanus, at the Abbey of St. Gall.

Still, opposition to the reform was not lacking, since some of the Gallican musicians were not at all favorable to the substitution of their chant with that of Rome, and this necessitated a compromise: they accepted the Roman texts and the modal structure of the melodies, but the Gallicans held the prerogative to preserve, wherever possible, the melody-types, to which they could apply newly adopted texts (for the orations, readings, and sometimes, the antiphons). In addition, they would also provide their own more elaborate type of ornamentation to the chants which had their own melodies.[8]

From this integration and melodic reworking of the Roman and Gallican liturgical and musical traditions emerged what is now

---

8. In Milan the Ambrosian musicians adapted a criterion analogous to that of the Gallicans to safeguard their musical tradition: they integrated their repertory, which was very limited (for example, there was only one formulary of chants for the Mass during all of the Easter season) with the Gregorian repertory, using an ornamentation that was typically Ambrosian.

commonly called Gregorian Chant.[9] The most ancient evidence of this new chant is found in the Tonary of Saint-Riquier (cod. Paris, Bibl. Nat. lat. 13159, eighth century). In this manuscript the chants are only documented by *incipit*,[10] and are laid out in the order of their mode.[11] Another century will pass before a musical notation will appear in the "books" of the new chant.

In the order in which they were redacted (eighth and ninth centuries), the first were the Antiphonaries of the Mass, with the documentation of sung texts only. Following these (tenth and eleventh centuries) were again the same, together with the Antiphonaries of the Office, but now with the addition of a-linear neumes, (*open field*[12]), and later, of neumes placed diastematically with or without a musical staff.

This documentation of chants on parchment marks the transition between two civilizations: one of "memory," which for nine centuries was the only form of transmission of liturgical chant, to one of "writing." It was thanks to the advent of notation that the dissemination of Gregorian Chant was able to occur so rapidly, as it would not have been possible within the sphere of the oral

---

9. Two clarifications: (1) Traces of infiltration and assimilation attributable to other liturgical and musical traditions, such as Beneventan or Mozarabic, are nowhere to be found in the Gregorian repertory, with the exception of Ambrosian. (2) The assignment of authorship of Gregorian Chant to Pope Gregory the Great (d. 604), due to his great fame as a reformer, and which was maintained throughout the Middle Ages, is without historical foundation. The term "Gregorian" does not trace back to him, but rather to the manuscript sources named "Gregorian," since it is in these that the formularies and their relative texts of the feasts were in accordance with the "Gregorian" calendar of the eighth century.

10. The first word, or words, of a chant used to designate it in its entirety.

11. The *tonary* emerges to facilitate the individuation of the mode and its relative psalm tone for the chants of both the Office and of the Mass. To this end, the first tonaries list only the verbal and melodic *incipits* of the chants, grouping them in one of the modes of the *octoechos* in which they belong. The later tonaries, especially those of the period of the Gregorian sources containing complete musical notation, extend the documentation to the entire composition.

12. Cf. chapter 1, footnote 4.

tradition. The ninth century is considered the period of demarcation between the classical and postclassical Gregorian repertories.

From the tenth to the thirteenth century, other musical forms were developed, such as the sequences, tropes, and hymns; the chants of the Kyriale that evolved and multiplied in both the semiornate and ornate genres; and Offices for new feasts and, even more so, for regional celebrations. For many of these compositions the authors of the texts are known, but the authors of the melodies, only very rarely.

In the seventeenth and eighteenth centuries compositions were created in "Gregorian style" (pseudo-Gregorian): for instance, the Masses[13] and the responsorial chant *Rorate Caeli* of Henry Du Mont (1610–1684); the Marian antiphon *Salve Regina* (simple tone) of Fr. François Bourgoing (1585–1610) reworked by Dom Joseph Pothier (VAT). Beyond the rhythmic-verbal understanding common to Gregorian, the composition of these pieces is marked by tonality, with an ornamentation and melodic shapes foreign to the classical Gregorian repertory.

Finally came the "neo-Gregorian" compositions of the twentieth century, using modal types and centonized formulas, created for particular celebrations of the dioceses.

3. The Gregorian repertory

The Gregorian repertory consists of a vast compilation of chants, whose multiplicity and heterogeneity of melodies is due to the musical forms, to the melodic genres, and to the various periods of composition. The source of all the Gregorian musical forms is found in that most ancient and basic liturgical unit, common to every celebration, that is, when there was still no distinction between the Mass and the Office. They are: readings, psalmody, and

---

13. In the Appendix of the 1960 edition of the *Liber Usualis*, three Masses of H. Du Mont, each containing also a *Credo,* can be found: the *Missa Regia,* 1; the *Missa 2i toni,* 5, and the *Missa 6i toni,* 10.

orations (prayers). Tertullian witnesses to their primitive existence in the second century: "whether it be in the reading of Scriptures, the chanting of psalms, the preaching of sermons, or in the offering up of prayers" (*De anima*, IX, 4). Two of these forms, the prayers and the readings, were entrusted to the celebrant and the minister, respectively; the third (psalmody) was entrusted to the cantor.

From the development of psalmody came the following liturgical-musical forms: in the Mass: the Tract, the Gradual and the Offertory; and in the Office: the Responsory[14] and the Antiphon.[15] In these forms the verses of the psalm still represent the principal part, and they require a specialist for their performance, whereas the refrains

---

14. In GREG there are two kinds of responsory: the *brief responsory*, and the *prolix responsory*. The difference between these two is not in the musical form, but in their melodic length: the first is a syllabic or semi-ornate genre, the second is an ornate genre. The reason for this different ornamentation is strictly related to the period of the year in which they are sung. The Rule of St. Benedict, chapter 10, prescribes the use of the brief response in the summer because the nights are brief: "From Easter till the calends of November let the whole psalmody, as explained above, be said, except that on account of the shortness of the nights, no lessons are read from the book; but instead of these three lessons, let one from the Old Testament be said from memory. Let a short responsory follow this."

15. The antiphon, which originated from the refrain of responsorial psalmody, has changed its melodic associations in the course of the history of the liturgy because of the nature of its texts. They range from antiphons with psalm texts that refer to, or are taken from, the psalm to which it is attached. These can be antiphons with brief texts, from the ferial Office, often taken from the beginning of the psalm or from its most characteristic verse, and with a melody of syllabic genre. Others are antiphons with reference to a feast (those of the most ancient feasts with longer texts and, sometimes, with melodies of semi-ornate genre). Others have non-psalmic Biblical texts, ecclesiastical or historical texts, some of which reflect in their text an episode in the life of a saint. There are also "independent" antiphons of semi-ornate genre not associated with alternation of verses of a psalm (for instance the *O Antiphon* of Advent, or the antiphons with texts derived from Byzantine tropes: *Sub tuum præsidium, Adorna thalamum tuum,* etc.; the Marian Antiphons: *Salve Regina, Alma Redemptoris Mater,* etc.; and the antiphons *per viam* that were sung during the processions of certain feasts, such as the Palm Sunday procession).

to the verses are a secondary part, easily learned from memory by the assembly. Later, the schola will take the place of the assembly with melodically more ornate compositions.

Closely related to the preceding, the liturgy introduced other forms along the course of its history, particularly, the *introit* and the *communion*. Their affinity with the previous forms is represented by the combination of antiphon with multiple psalm verses. In these, however, the antiphon constitutes the principal part, and, as such, requires specialized performers; whereas the psalm verse becomes almost a pretext for the repetition of the antiphon. The Alleluia of the Mass constitutes its own musical form: it appears a century before St. Gregory the Great (d. 604) as a chant acclamation sung by the schola after the gospel, without a verse and in melismatic style.

Other liturgical-musical forms—the litany, the acclamation and the hymns—have their distant roots in the orations and in psalmody. The litany and the acclamation are connected to the orations of the celebrant and to the intercessions of the deacon, and from the development of these follow, respectively, the melodies of the *Kyrie,* the *Sanctus,* and, at the end of the seventh century, of the *Agnus Dei.*

Finally, from the ancient psalm tones come hymnody, from which will evolve the melodies of the *Gloria* and of the *Credo.*

Some mention has already been made about the melodic genres of the above musical forms. In brief, it can be said that Gregorian musical forms were elaborated in three different melodic genres: syllabic, semi-ornate, and ornate or melismatic. This is with respect to the nature of the texts, to their place in worship, and in relation to the minister of the celebration.

In the syllabic genre, to every syllable of text corresponds, for the most part, a single note. In this genre an absolute preeminence is given to the text. In the semi-ornate genre the syllables are ornamented by small groups of two or three notes. In this genre, a more melodic and poetic one, the text is given the possibility of expressing itself with more developed, lyric accents. In ornate or melismatic genre the syllables are embellished with a real flowering of notes. These are vocalizations that are articulated musically, but not textually, and they compensate for the expressive absence of text with the force and power of melody.

Another aspect of the Gregorian repertory that cannot be neglected concerns the origins of the chants from various liturgical-musical traditions. Many and varied studies have been published, and current research continues on the relationship of these liturgical repertories, all contributing to the growth of our body of knowledge. For instance, the presence or absence of a chant in one of the Antiphonaries of the *Sextuplex*[16] constitutes a fundamental indication regarding its provenance. More to the point though, it is in light of the history of the liturgy, connected to the history of the musical composition—for these two realities proceed in parallel—that emerge the most decisive data. Here are some examples that illustrate the variety of melodic-modal styles of three liturgical-musical traditions. Many of the pieces from the liturgical period of Advent were imported from the Gallican tradition: the melody-type of the Antiphons in *protus-deuterus* in A, 2*—Mode IV (p. 200 ex. A.12), the Graduals in Mode II in A (p. 201 ex. A.13), and the Tracts in RE of Holy Week (p. 202 ex. A.14). Of Roman origin are the compositions of the Tracts in SOL (Mode VIII) from the season of Lent (p. 204 ex. A.15). Finally, from the Gregorian Period come the compositions of the Canticles of the Easter Vigil in *tetrardus,* Mode VIII (p. 205 ex. A.16).

Another example concerns liturgical celebrations of a saint, connected to a specific territory. These were characterized, as would be expected, by compositions whose modal structures

---

16. The *Sextuplex* (= *Antiphonale Missarum Sextuplex,* Rome 1935) is a publication edited by Dom René-Jean Hesbert, monk of Solesmes, in which are synoptically displayed the texts of chants (at the time of its compilation neumatic notation was not yet well understood) in six manuscripts, one *Cantatorium*, and five *Graduali*, dated from the eighth to the ninth centuries. Ex. A11 (Appendix pages 198–199) reproduce an example of a synoptic table.

mirror the local musical traditions. Compare, for instance, the antiphons of Pope St. Clement I, a feast of Roman origins, with those of the Conversion of St. Paul, a feast of Gallican origin: the first antiphons have the melody of the modal templates of MI and of DO, originating in the Roman-Gregorian tradition, while the others have melodics of two modal templates of RE, originating in the Gallican-Gregorian tradition (p. 207 ex. A.18).

4. The relevance of Gregorian chant

Beyond its primary and essential quality as sung prayer, Gregorian chant is celebrated as having a profound religiosity. Up to the present day it is the only chant that has embodied the most genuine and ancient spirit of Christian faith in the West, being the fruit of a matured experience of communal prayer and choral practice. For these two reasons the Church of Rome has always declared Gregorian monody as her very own chant.

One of the innovative provisions of the Second Vatican Council in the field of liturgy was the admission of modern, spoken languages in the liturgical celebrations (SC 54). Following this, Gregorian chant, for the fact of being strictly tied to its Latin text, suffered a sharp downturn, notwithstanding the fact that Latin remains, in the spirit of the conciliar Constitution, the official language of the liturgy: "The use of the Latin language, except when a particular law prescribes otherwise, is to be preserved in the Latin rites" (SC 36). The Instruction *Musicam sacram* of the Sacred Congregation of Rites for the application of the conciliar norms (1967), states:

> In sung liturgical services celebrated in Latin: (a) Gregorian chant, as proper to the Roman liturgy, should be given pride of place, other things being equal. Its melodies, contained in the "typical" editions, should be used, to the extent that this is possible. (b) "It is also desirable that an edition be prepared containing simpler melodies, for use in smaller churches." (c) Other musical settings, written for one or more voices, be they

taken from the traditional heritage or from new works, should be held in honor, encouraged and used as the occasion demands. (MS 50)

In compliance with these provisions, it is clear that the Constitution strongly recommends musical education in liturgical chant for musicians, cantors, and in particular for children, to preserve the patrimony of sacred music and to encourage the new forms of sacred chant. "Much emphasis should be placed on the teaching of music and on musical activity in seminaries, in the novitiates and houses of studies of religious of both sexes, and also in other Catholic institutions and schools" (SC 115). For this reason, "the study and practice of Gregorian chant is to be promoted, because, with its special characteristics, it is a basis of great importance for the development of sacred music" (MS 52).

The introduction of modern, spoken languages should not be assessed negatively, even though it resulted in the decline of Gregorian chant practice. It is right that different periods and cultures contribute to the realization of liturgical repertories, just as it has been in the past. Moreover, it should be recalled that a good part of the Gregorian repertory was not composed for an average liturgical assembly, but for specialized ensembles: a *schola* or monastic community. To have pretended, in these last few decades, to entrust to everyone the singing of the *Graduale Romanum*, has resulted in unsatisfactory renditions from both a cultural and a religious perspective. With the aim of encouraging the singing of the liturgy in Latin, even in smaller churches, the liturgical reform, according to the conciliar requirements, has provided for an edition of the *Kyriale Simplex* and of the *Graduale Simplex*, to place alongside the *Graduale Romanum* (cf. SC 117 and MS 50/b). With both these editions available, one for the people and one for the schola, one can draw freely, even in the same celebration, from the ornate repertory and from the simpler repertory of the new books. Regulations such as these provide for an effective enhancement of Gregorian chant: every assembly is offered, without any imposition, the possibility to access a repertory that is appropriate to its own interpretive capacities.

Beyond the considerations of a liturgical and a pastoral nature, no one questions the extraordinary cultural fact represented by Gregorian chant. It constitutes a monument and patrimony of inestimable value. Hundreds of manuscripts, spread throughout the principal libraries of Europe, are the nearly exclusive depositaries of primitive musical notation. Thousands of Latin texts, from those created to ornament the musical forms of the classical repertory up until the tropes, sequences, and hymns, constitute the quasi totality of medieval Latin literature.

The perfect symbiosis of word and melody, expressed by the ornamentation of the various melodic genres; the rhythmic technique deduced from the articulation of the syllables in the context of the word and of the phrase; the wealth and strength of the melodies, simple and natural in their meanderings through modal structures; afford the refined and fascinating creative synthesis that is Gregorian chant, the fruit of religious experience and artistic maturity. It has been due to the sciences of paleography and semiology, as well as to those relative to modality that these fundamental aspects of Gregorian chant have come to light.

CHAPTER 1

THE SOURCES

1. Manuscript sources

In the history of any language, whether spoken or musical, practice always precedes notation. And so it was for Gregorian monody, the documentation of which dates from the beginning of the tenth century. The need to transition from the oral tradition to a written, notated tradition does not apply to the Gallican repertory, but rather to the new repertory mandated by the Carolingian reform with the adoption of the Roman liturgy. Its dissemination required the support of notation. It would have been of concern with the Roman chant, but in reality, that was nothing other than a hybrid of Old Roman and Gallican chant. The process of consigning the chant to parchment proceeded in phases. First came the documentation of the texts of the chants alone, and in a second phase the documentation also extended to musical notation.

On page 208 (ex. A.19) is a folio from the *Graduale* of Corbie (cod. Paris, Bibl. Nat., lat. 12050), dated ninth century, after 853. Although it has no musical notation, this manuscript contains important references regarding the modality of certain pieces. In the left margin, at the level of the Introit and Communion antiphons' *incipit*, are the abbreviations of their psalm tones. They are as follows:

AP (*authenticus protus*)   = Mode I psalm tone
PP (*plagis proti*)   = Mode II psalm tone

AD (*authenticus deuterus*)   = Mode III psalm tone
PD (*plagis deuterus*)   = Mode IV psalm tone
ATR (*authenticus tritus*)   = Mode V psalm tone
PTR (*plagis triti*)   = Mode VI psalm tone
ATE (*authenticus tetrardus*)   = Mode VII psalm tone
PTE (*plagis tetrardus*)   − Mode VIII psalm tone

The Antiphonary (*Graduale*) of Corbie is one of the six manuscripts of the *Sextuplex*. With their respective abbreviations, they list as:

M   *Cantatorium* of Monza (ca. the first half of the ninth century)
R   *Graduale* of Rheinau (ca. 800)
B   *Graduale* of Mont-Blandin (eighth–ninth centuries)
C   *Graduale* of Compiègne (second half of the ninth century)
K   *Graduale* of Corbie (after the year 853)
S   *Graduale* of Senlis (last quarter of the ninth century)

The chants with texts present in one of the six manuscripts of the *Sextuplex* are considered the Gregorian *classical* repertory. In the GT, at the beginning of each piece, appears the manuscript abbreviation(s) in which it is recorded.

The documentation of the melodies also proceeded in phases. The first to receive musical notation were the chants of the Mass for the readings in ornate (melismatic) genre—Canticles, Tracts, Graduals, Alleluias—all of which were notated in manuscripts entitled *Cantatorium*.

In the second phase were the chants in semi-ornate genre that accompany processions in the Mass—Introits, Offertories, Communions—notated in the manuscripts entitled *Graduale*. These manuscripts also include the chants for the readings since they too are part of the repertory for the Mass entrusted to the schola. Consequently, the birth of the *Graduale* signified a decline for the *Cantatorium*.

Finally, came the documentation of the Office chants in both syllabic genre: Antiphons and brief Responsories; and semi-ornate genre: Prolix Responsories, all of which appear in manuscripts entitled *Antiphonale*.

Next to these, other manuscripts were created in response to particular ritual needs:

the *Missale*, with all of the texts needed for the celebration of the Mass. Along with the texts set to music in the *Graduale*, it includes the Readings, Orations, Eucharistic Prayer, etc.

the *Versicularium*, with the psalm verses for the Introit and Communion processional chants; the *Troparium* with the tropes of the chants of the *Ordinarium*[1] and, occasionally, the sequences and liturgical dramas

the *Sequentiarium*, with the sequences

the *Tonarium*, with the chants of the *Proprium*, grouped and arranged according to the modes of the *octoechos*

Concerning the Office there were:

the *Breviarium*, liturgically parallel to the *Missale* and containing the chants of the *Antiphonale* and the texts of the readings

the *Psalterium*, with the texts of the Psalms, and, occasionally, the melodies of the Antiphons

the *Hymnarius*, with the melodies of the Hymns

Finally, are the *Corali*, manuscripts of large dimensions containing only parts of, or a limited selection of, the chants of the Mass or the Office; they are in square notation on four lines, and often decorated with rich miniature illuminations.

---

1. The chants of the *Proprium*, whose texts change from one Mass to another, include the chants for the readings (Canticle, Tract, Graduale, Alleluia) and the chants that accompany a procession: at the beginning of the celebration (Introit), at the presentation of the gifts (Offertory), and at communion (Communio). The chants of the *Ordinarium* include those whose texts do not change from one Mass to another: *Kyrie, Gloria, Credo, Sanctus,* and *Agnus Dei.*

As stated above, the first Gregorian manuscript sources with musical notation appear at the beginning of the tenth century, that is, one century after the composition of the Gregorian repertory. In this period of time, the first attempts at notation were made using signs traced in the margins of liturgical documents of text only. They were derived from common grammatical signs indicating acute and grave accents (p. 209 ex. A.20), used by grammarians to express the melodic aspect of the proclamation of a literary text.[2] The Gregorian musicians considered them apt to express the natural sense of the melody. The acute accent, whose sign was given the name *virga*, indicates an ascending melodic line; the grave accent, whose sign received the name *punctum*, indicates a descending melodic line. These two signs combine in various ways to create more complex signs.

The *virga* and *punctum*, and the signs derived from their combination, were traced at first above the text, in "open field" (*campo aperto*), that is, displayed upon a horizontal line drawn "*a secco*."[3]

From this come the phrases *adiastematic neumes* [4] and *adiastematic neumatic notation*, because the neumes do not provide an exact intervallic distance between the sounds. Nonetheless, they were

2. The topic of accents is treated in more detail in chapter 2 beginning on page 71.

3. Horizontal lines were drawn on the parchments of the codices to facilitate the alignment of the texts. These were traced not with liquid (ink) but with a dry clay substance, like a pencil. In order to facilitate the musical notation, it became the practice to write the texts on every other line. In this way, the line of the empty space became a kind of guide so that the musical signs were also aligned.

4. νεύω, from which comes νεῦμα, that literally means "to bow" as in "bowing one's head," but in a derived sense of the word, meaning "to hint, to allude." The signs, drawn in "open field," do not exactly express the intervals between sounds, but they only *hint, allude* to them. For this they are called *neumes*. Since the word *neume* is also used to indicate signs that do specify melodic intervals, the term is sometimes combined with the adjectives "*adiastematic,*" from ἀ-διαστηματικός, and "*diastematic*" from διαστηματικός. *Adiastematic neumes* are those without distinct reference to melodic intervals; and *diastematic neumes* are those which have distinct reference to intervals.

sufficiently clear to provide a rough drawing of the melody. Later, to graphically indicate the acoustic distance between tones, they became *diastematic* neumes placed above the text, at first without, then with, a line. Gradually, other types of notation emerged using, primarily, small *punctums* rather than accent signs. This change responded to a preference to obtain a more precise diastemacy with the neumatic signs, especially when using lined parchment.[5]

The adiastematic musical notation of the manuscript sources belonging to European scriptoria distant from one another, and dated nearly contemporaneously, reveals a surprising fact. Notwithstanding the different semiographic style of the place to which they belong, the manuscripts possess a remarkable compositional and expressive uniformity. The science of paleography has subdivided the various neumatic notations in roughly fifteen families. Examples of some of these, in chronological order of the evolution of their notation, from adiastematic to diastematic, are as follows:

1. Paleographic musical notation of St. Gall:[6] cod. St-Gallen, Stiftsbibl. 359, beginning of the tenth century, *Cantatorium* (p. 210 ex. A.21). This codex contains only the chants for the readings; for the other chants the *incipit* is given. The adiastematic notation is traced on a horizontal plane, inclined toward the right, and with a subtle, delicate *ductus* of the pen. The neumes give a diagram of the melodic line and the structure of the composition; for the melody, the cantor must refer to the oral tradition. This manuscript was published in PM II/2 and MPG 3.

2. Paleographic musical notation of St. Gall: cod. Einsiedeln, Stiftsbibl. 121, between the years 964–971, *Graduale* of the monastic library of Einsiedeln (p. 211 ex. A.22). The most ancient

---

5. Cf. pp. 220–221.

6. The geographical area of the St. Gall paleographic family includes German Switzerland and southern Bavaria, with branches in northern Italy, especially Monza, and Bobbio. It contains the largest number of manuscripts with adiastematic notation due to the fact that the scriptorium of the monastery of St. Gall maintained this notation even after the advent of musical notation on lines.

manuscript from St. Gall with musical notation for all of the chants of the Mass, it contains the Introit, Offertory and Communion processional chants, and the chants of the readings, previously codified in the *Cantatorium*. The abundant use of letters added to the paleographic neumes confirms the hypothesis that this manuscript was produced for the learning of the chants by the schola. It was published in PM I/4 and in a facsimile reproduction, *Graduale und Sequenzen Notkers von St. Gallen* (Weinheim: VCH, Acta Humaniora, 1991).

3. Paleographic musical notation of Metz (*metense*) or, more precisely, of Lorraine (*lorenese*):[7] cod. Laon, Bibl.Mun. 239, from close to the year 930, *Graduale* (p. 212 ex. A.23). It is the only exemplar of this type of notation that we possess. Though it has no staff lines, the notation is quasi-diastematic. The writing of the neumes is particularly accurate: the signs are traced with a vertical movement and with flexibility of the pen. The manuscript was published in PM I/10.

4. French paleographic musical notation: cod. Mont-Renaud, second half of the tenth century, *Graduale-Antiphonale* of Saint-Éloi de Noyon[8] (p. 213 ex. A.24). It is a double "*Antiphonale*"—for the Mass, *Graduale* (pp. 1–48) (fols. 1–48v), and for the Office (fols. 49r–129). It is likely that this was originally two separate manuscripts and intended to contain only the texts. This assumption stems from the fact that there is not enough space for the musical

---

7. The designation "of Metz" is in relation to the city of Metz, which was considered the seat of the *scriptorium* of this notation. In reality, the best witness of this notation, as in the indicated codex, comes from the Cathedral of Laon, the capital of ancient Austrasia, now part of the region of Lorraine. For this reason the designation of the paleographic notation of *Lorraine*, or "*lorenese*," is more appropriate: cf. S. Corbin, *Die Neumen*, vol. 1 fasc. 3 of *Palaeographie der Musik* (Köln: Volk, 1977), 3, 87. The paleographic musical notation of Lorraine was geographically extended to the northeast of France and Belgium, with influence also in Italy, especially at Como and Vercelli.

8. This manuscript was discovered by Abbot Eugène Müller in the Castle of Mont-Renaud, an ancient Charterhouse of Notre-Dame, near Noyon.

notation between the lines of text, which is, therefore, very compressed, and frequently goes beyond the space above the words and into the margins, becoming somewhat illegible and disordered. It was published in PM I/16, 1955, and 1989.

5. Beneventan[9] paleographic musical notation: cod. Benevento, Bibl. Cap. 33, tenth-eleventh centuries, *Missale Antiquum*, in adiastematic notation (p. 214 ex. A.25). This codex is incomplete since it begins with the Vigil of Christmas, rather than with the first Sunday of Advent. The scribe worked with a beaked pen, tracing the signs vertically and horizontally and somewhat thickly. The ligatures between the neumatic elements occurred by dragging the pen along the parchment, with frequent curls. Often, the latter will indicate the presence of a *liquescence*.[10] It is published in PM I/20 and in MPG 1.

6. Cod. Benevento, Bibl. 40, beginning of the eleventh century, *Graduale*, with diastematic notation in fragments, without lines (p. 215 ex. A.26). It is the most ancient of the Beneventan manuscripts, but is incomplete, beginning with Monday of Holy Week. It is published in CG 1.

7. Cod. Benevento, Bibl. 34, eleventh-twelfth centuries, *Graduale*, with diastematic notation on two lines with letter clefs (p. 216

---

9. The geographical center of Beneventan notation includes Benevento, Montecassino, and Bari. However, its influence also extended through the region of Campania to Rome. The Beneventan manuscripts rigorously preserved the psalmodic tenor on the note SI of authentic *deuterus*, Mode III, and, in the psalmody of the Office, the psalmodic tenor on SOL of plagal *deuterus*, Mode IV. Moreover, they maintained the scale degrees of MI and SI in the compositional contexts that, in the Gregorian codices, regularly slid up to FA and to DO.

10. *Liquescence* is a semiological-phonetic phenomenon that results from the complex articulation of certain syllables—for example, with the meeting of two consonants, or with a diphthong in the passage between syllables—in the correct diction of a text. In fact, this articulation produces a *transitory position* in the vocal organs such that the sound is diminished or almost swallowed. Thus, the origin of "liquescent" is found in the Latin verb *liquefacere* (to dissolve). *Semivocalis* or *hemivocalis*, followed by the expression *sive substringes*. See P. M. Ferretti, *Principi teorici e pratici di canto gregoriano* (Rome: Desclée, 1914), 79.

ex. A.27).[11] It is the only complete Gradual in the Capitular Library of Benevento, and for this reason it was chosen to be published in PM I/15.

8. Paleographic musical notation of Northeastern Central Italy: cod. Roma, Bibl. Angelica 123 (B. 3.18), beginning of eleventh century, *Graduale-Troparium* of Bologna (p. 243 ex. A.28). The notation is adiastematic, very similar to the script of Nonantola. In fact, the neumes are traced almost obliquely, reaching down toward the letters of the text to which they refer. It is published in PM I/18.

9. Breton[12] paleographic musical notation: cod. Chartres 47, tenth century, *Graduale*. (p. 244 ex. A.29). From a scriptorium of one of the monasteries of Brittany, probably Saint-Sauveur de Redon, it traveled to the monastery of Saint-Père-en-Vallée near the city of Chartres in the eleventh century.[13] The original codex was destroyed in a fire on May 26, 1944, during a bombing of the Second World War. Fortunately, we possess a reproduction of the precious manuscript published in 1912 as volume XI of PM. This *Graduale* is an adiastematic manuscript representing the connecting link between the Paleofrankish and the Aquitanian notations, its notation presenting somewhat simplified accents. Beyond the

11. The use of clefs at the beginning of the staff lines to indicate the acoustic position of the notes was preceded chronologically by the use of alphabetic letter musical notation. The letters most frequently used were those for DO and FA, corresponding to the strong tones, below which are found the semitone. The reading of the other notes is facilitated in reference to the position of these. In some manuscript sources the use of other letters can be found: *a* for the line indicating LA below DO, and *d* for the line indicating RE underneath FA.

12. This notation is centered in Brittany, in northwestern France, but it extends beyond the English Channel to Cornwall and to the neighboring regions of Normandy.

13. Cf. G. Benoit-Castelli and M. Huglo, "L'origine bretonne du Graduel 47 de la Bibliothèque de Chartres," *Études Grégoriennes* 1 (1954): 173–178.

view of the musical notation, there are indications regarding the
initial, mediant and final notes of the pieces.[14]

10. French paleographic musical notation: cod. Montpellier,
Bibl. de la Faculté de Médecine H. 159, eleventh century, *Graduale-
Tonarium*, in double notation, adiastematic and alphabetic (p. 219
ex. A.30) The alphabetic notation uses a system of letters from
a–p, with an extension of two octaves.

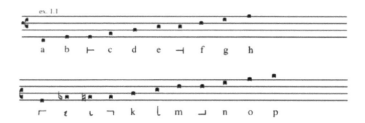

The manuscript is published in PM I/8, 1901–1905. It has also been
transcribed onto a four-line staff and published in F. E. Hansen,
H. 159 Montpellier: Tonary of St. Bénigne of Dijon (Kopenhagen:
D. Fog musikforlag, 1974).

11. Aquitanian[15] paleographic musical notation: cod. Paris,
Bibl. Nat. lat. 776, second half of the eleventh century, *Graduale-
Troparium* of the Abbey of Saint-Michel Gaillac, belonging to
the diocese of Albi. From this comes its normal designation as
codex Albi (p. 220 ex. A.31). It is a complete *Graduale*, but also
contains prosule, prose, and processional chants. The notation of
this manuscript is diastematic, with lines drawn *a secco* for both
the text and the neumatic notation. Pinhole guides, in circular or in
elongated form and traced outside of the writing space determine

14. Cf. K. Pouderoijen, "L'interprétation des indications du Graduel 47," in
*Requirentes modos musicos: mélanges offerts à Dom Jean Claire, à l'occasion de
son 75ᵉ anniversaire, de ses 50 ans de profession monastique et de ses 25 ans comme
Maître de chœur à Solesmes*," ed. D. Saulnier (Solesmes, 1995), 261–274.

15. It extends to the southwest of ancient Gaul, in the territory of Languedoc,
with influence toward the southeast.

the distance between the lines. The neumatic signs are short with frequent use of *punctum* both isolated and in composition. The reciting tone, or *tenor,* of the Mode III psalm tone, has already risen from SI to DO. It was published in CG 3.

12. Cod. Paris, Bibl. Nat. Lat. 903, *Graduale* of St-Yrieix, near Limoges, eleventh century, in diastematic notation, with lines drawn *a secco,* but without letter clefs (p. 221 ex. A.32). The line *a secco* facilitates the reading of the notes because its placement takes into account the modality of the piece. The melodies in authentic mode place the line higher than the final note, at the interval of a third. For those in plagal mode, the line *a secco* coincides with the scale degree of the final, with the exception of *plagal deuterus,* for which the line *a secco* corresponds to FA. The scale degrees of the line *a secco* are as follows:

mode	authentic	plagal
protus	FA	RE
deuterus	SOL	FA, in place of MI
tritus	LA	FA
tetrardus	SI	SOL

The manuscript is published in PM I/13.

13. Paleographic musical notation of Central Italy: cod. Lucca, Bibl. Cap 601, twelfth century, *Antiphonale Monasticum,* in diastematic notation on two lines with letter clefs (p. 222 ex. A.33), published in PM I/9.

14. German, with influence of Metz paleographic musical notation: cod. Graz, Univ. 807, second half of the twelfth century, *Graduale* of Klosterneuberg, in diastematic notation on two colored lines: a red line indicates FA, and a yellow line indicates DO (p. 223 ex. A.34). It also uses letter clefs: C to indicate DO, A to indicate LA, D to indicate RE. This manuscript is published in PM I/19.

15. English square notation on four lines, with clefs: cod. Worcester, F. 160, *Antiphonale Monasticum,* thirteenth century (p. 224 ex. A.35), published in PM I/12.

2. Alphabetic notation

Paleographic notation, of which some of the more significant examples have just been presented, was not the only musical notation in existence since the ninth century. Instructional works by medieval musicians also contain an alphabetic musical notation, already in use in ancient Greece. This type of notation was not invented to substitute for neumatic notation, nor was the latter invented to take the place of the alphabetic. The neumatic and the alphabetic are two different notations intended to document the melodies, each of which has its own character and objective: the alphabetic notation, to determine the pitches of the scale; the neumatic notation, to represent the melodic formulas. The two notations were able to exist contemporaneously and complement one another.[16]

Medieval musicians adapted *in toto* the alphabetic notation of the Greeks, substituting the Greek letters for Latin ones, after a time, and applying them to the pitches of musical instruments as well as to the diatonic scale degrees of vocal music.[17] The note LA grave represented the first degree of the scale, that is, below the median note. This first degree was indicated with capital A, the second with capital B, and so on until the highest note of the scale, the fifteenth, with capital P. Some authors, however, propose repeating the first letter of the alphabet after the seventh scale degree, since the pitches repeat in the same order of whole tones and semitones. But, so as not to confuse the sounds of the lower octave with those of the higher octave, they adopt the lowercase letters of the alphabet for the first octave and the doubling of these for the second octave.[18]

---

16. Cf. cod. Montpellier, Bibl. de la Faculté de Médecine H. 159, p. 245.

17. On the monochord the letters of the alphabet were applied in correspondence to the various bridges that were moved along the instrument along a line divided into equal parts. With other instruments the letters were applied to the various strings and their relative bridges.

18. Cf. p. 226 ex. A.37.

Another musical notation that has many analogies to the alphabetic one is *daseian* notation (p. 225 ex. A.36). Certain treatises use this notation, most notably the *Musica enchiriadis* and the *Commemoratio brevis*, attributed to Hucbald of Saint-Amand (c. 840–930). Its name derives from the sign that forms the basis of the notation, the *dasian* (from the Greek δασέα, "aspirated sign"), a slanted stick upon which is drawn at the halfway point a smaller line, resembling half of a letter H, an aspirated alphabetic letter. Above and below the oblique stick, on the right or left, is a line with modifications of the pen's *ductus* to distinguish the four tetrachords arranged in ascending order, and forms the musical diagram of fifteen pitches used by medieval theoreticians: two ascending octaves (LA–LA), to which are added a lower note (SOL) and the movable note (*pien*).

On page 226 (ex. A.37) there is the complete diagram of pitches proposed by medieval theoreticians, subdivided in ascending tetrachords, with the semitone in the center of each tetrachord. Below this are four alphabetic notations: the alphabetic notation of the theorists, the notation of the Montpellier codex, the alphabetic notation used by the monk Guido d'Arezzo, and, finally, the daseian notation.

The musicians of the late Middle Ages used yet another system to indicate intervals. They placed the syllables of the text in between lines to give each its intended intonation. At the beginning of each line is the letter S or T, indicating if the interval is a semitone or a whole tone (p. 227 ex. A.38). This type of notation immediately precedes the advent of notation on the musical staff, in which the notes come to substitute the syllables of the text and are placed directly on the lines.

3. Historical overview of the printed editions

The printed editions of Gregorian chant, including those from the sixteenth century to the present, can be grouped in three periods: the editions from the period of decline, those from before the "Vatican" restoration, and those from after the "Vatican" restoration.

Foremost of the first period's editions is the infamous *Medicea* edition of 1614, containing substantially altered melodies, and which for three centuries held unchallenged dominion, contributing more than any other factor to the decline of Gregorian chant. Rendered nearly "official" by Pope Paul V in 1622, it was revived in 1870 by the Pustet editions of Regensburg, with a thirty-year exclusive approbation of the Holy See. A comparison of the restored melodic version of VAT with that of the Pustet version of the Communion *Viderunt omnes* (p. 228 ex. A.39) will illustrate the severity of damage perpetrated by this edition concerning the Gregorian repertory. Compare also the metamorphosis of the *Alleluia, Omnes gentes* in a series of nine editions of Gregorian chant, beginning with that of Pustet from 1871 (pp. 229–230 ex. A.40). Included are the melodic versions of the following editions:

1. *Medicean Gradual* of 1614

2. *Reims/Cambrai Gradual* of 1852, p. 277, edited by Cardinals Gousset and Giraud, archbishops of Reims and of Cambrai, respectively

3. *Parisian Gradual* of 1857, p. 292, published in Paris under the name of P. Lambillotte, posth. (n. 3)[19]

4. *Solesmes Gradual* of 1883, p. 334, edited by Dom Joseph Pothier

5. *Liber Usualis*, Solesmes, 1903, p. 287, edited by Dom André Mocquereau

6. *Graduale Romanum*, edition *typica* of 1908, p. 287, edited by Dom Joseph Pothier

7. *Graduale Romanum, ad exemplar editionis typicae concinnatum et rhythmicis signis a Solesmensibus monachis diligenter ornatum*, p. 313

19. Cf. A. Gastoué, *Le graduel et l'antiphonaire romains: histoire et description*, Musique et liturgie (Lyon: Janin, 1913).

8. *Graduale Romanum, Pauli PP. VI* of 1974, p. 298

9. *Graduale Triplex seu Graduale Romanum Pauli PP. VI* of 1974–1979, p. 298

The first three melodic versions, of which the first is in *protus* and the other two in *deuterus*, are very strange: the melodies, though they contain many characteristic elements of the manuscript sources, are simplified in a way even more imaginative than the editions of the seventeenth century. The melodic versions that follow, beginning with 4, translate the neumes from the adiastematic manuscript sources onto the staff with greater precision. Nevertheless, two details in these versions underline the progressive refinements in notation regarding the use of bar lines for the subdivisions of phrasing, and the introduction of certain signs regarding rhythmic interpretation.

In versions 4 and 5, a double bar is placed after the melodic fragment *a*, indicating that the intonation of the alleluia phrase, sung by a soloist, would be repeated by the schola before all continue with fragment *b*. In versions 6 and 7, a similar interruption of the *iubilus* for the repetition of the *alleluia* is indicated, but, more correctly, *after* the melodic fragment *b*.

The second detail relates to fragment *c* (the *porrectus* neume), which in 6 and 7 is considered a cadential element and not a beginning element of the *iubilus*. The double bar and the half bar (of the previous versions) have been replaced by the quarter bar; the final notes of the incise and the note that begins the *iubilus* are dotted; and, finally, the *clivis* neume (after *c*) is topped with the horizontal *episema* sign as in the manuscript sources.

Version 7 (VAT, of which Dom Pothier was the editor in charge) reintroduces the half bar, and fragment *c* returns again to the beginning of the incise.

In version 7, the vertical *episema* is introduced, outside of final syllables of words and of final melodic notes, to indicate the binary and ternary groupings.

Version 9 introduces the slur to correct the misplaced location of the half bar in the *iubilus*.

The period of the restoration of Gregorian chant begins at the Abbey of Saint-Pierre de Solesmes (France), under the driving force of abbot Dom Prosper Guéranger, and with the collaboration of a group of his monks. The restored melodies faithfully reproduce the neumes contained in the most reliable manuscripts, though their melodic versions still contain alternative readings. These melodies will form the basis of the future editions of the Vatican.

After the publication of the volume entitled *Méthode raisonnée de plain-chant* (1859) of the canon Augustin-Mathurin Gontier of Le Mans, which addressed the problem of rhythmic interpretation, abbot Guéranger had appointed Dom Paul Jausions (1834–1870) to prepare a restored edition of the Gregorian melodies based on approximately ten manuscript sources in the workshop (*l'atelier*) of the abbey. In this work Dom Jausions was joined by another monk, Dom Joseph Pothier (1835–1923). The first fruit of their collaboration was the publication, in 1880, of *Les mélodies grégoriennes d'après la tradition*. The volume came out, however, only with the name of Dom Pothier, because Dom Jausions had died around ten years prior. As before, attention was directed almost exclusively to show that "oratorical" rhythm would determine the melodic rhythm. In light of this presupposition, all those elements fostering a correct pronunciation of literary discourse led to the conclusion that this is the indispensable premise for a warm, supple, elegant interpretation of the melodies. The work also treats the argument of the origins of neumatic notation, offering a first synthesis of the discipline of *neumatics*.

Three years later, in 1883, Dom Pothier published his *Graduale*. In the evaluation of the Gregorian scholars, one could finally speak of an "authentic edition" of Gregorian chant, because his melodic versions truly reflected the tradition of the manuscript sources. Already one year earlier, at the Congress of Arezzo (1882), Dom Pothier had performed some melodies in the version of his *Graduale*, receiving such consensus that the attendees decided to abandon the *Medicea* version. On that occasion, a commission was promoted to recommend to Pope Leo XIII that Pothier's melodies receive approbation. Still, the Pope, though encouraging the work, did not think it opportune at that time to repudiate the edition of Regensburg.

After the *Graduale*, Dom Pothier endeavored to publish the books of chant of the Divine Office: the *Hymnarius* (1885), the Office *Ad Matutinam* of Christmas (1885), the Holy Week Triduum (1886), and the Office of the Dead (1887). In 1891 he published the *Antiphonale pro diurnis horis*, in a double version, according to both the monastic cursus and the Roman, and in 1895, the *Liber Responsorialis* according to the monastic rite, for the major feasts.

In 1896, the first editions of the *Liber Usualis Missæ et Officii* appeared, a practical publication that contained in one volume the chants of the Mass as well as those of the Office, for the principal Sundays and feasts, without having to resort to other liturgical books. The publication received such success throughout the world that five editions were produced between 1903 and 1905.

While Dom Pothier endeavored to arrive, one step at a time, at a complete edition of the melodies of the liturgical chant, another monk of Solesmes, Dom André Mocquereau (1849–1930), began the series *Paléographie Musicale* (PM), with reproductions in facsimile of the most authoritative Gregorian manuscripts. Dom Mocquereau had photographs made of a large number of codices from the principal libraries of Europe. These greatly augmented the workshop of Solesmes where the codices were studied. Many of their adiastematic and diastematic versions were comparatively transcribed on large *tableaux*, with a view toward a more scientifically credible edition. Dom Mocquereau introduced improvements to the *Graduale* of Dom Pothier in his reedition of the *Paroissien*, or *Liber Usualis*, of 1903, which, however, were not welcomed by the Pontifical Commission presided over by Dom Pothier. They determined that only the supplementary signs of the double bar, full bar, half bar and quarter bar would be added to the square notation of the melodies. Dom Mocquereau had introduced the quarter bar to make the phrasing of both the text and the melodies visible, and the other three had previously been in the *Graduale* of 1883. It was noted in the preface of this *Graduale*, that the system of rhythmic interpretation of the melodies was sufficiently represented by the so-called "white spaces" within the plurisonic neumes.[20]

The Pontifical Commission edited the following editions of the Vatican: the *Kyriale Romanum* (1905), with the melodies of the *Ordinarium Missæ*; the *Graduale Romanum* (1907, decree of approval; 1908, year of publication), containing the melodies of the *Proprium Missæ*; the *Antiphonale Romanum pro diurnis horis* (1912).

Beginning in 1913, the Holy See entrusted the Abbey of Solesmes with the continuing work of the restoration of the Gregorian melodies under the supervision of a consultant to the Congregation of Rites, in the person of abbot Paolo Ferretti, OSB. The editions that came to light in this second phase of the restoration of Gregorian chant are the *Officium Majoris Hebdomadæ et Octavæ Paschæ* (1922), and the Offices for Christmas (1926) and for the Dead

20. Dom J. Claire writes in this regard:
The members of the Vatican Commission were not opposed on principle to all rhythmic signs; but the heated, and not always correct, polemic, it must be said, prevented any constructive discussion. A pure and simple prohibition of any sign added to the Vatican edition, was loudly demanded, for according to their authors, it needed no other clarification than those contained in the preface. Now the preface also had its system of rhythmic signs, the famous 'white [spaces]' within the groups of notes, the interpretation of which was so difficult, that two of the authors of the edition and its preface, Peter Wagner and Amédée Gastoué having suggested to, each in his own way, translate into modern notation the very example proposed in their preface, (the end of Kyrie IX), they could not agree on the placement of the eighth notes and quarter notes! ("Un secolo di lavoro a Solesmes," *Studi Gregoriani* 16 [2000]: 28).

Ky- ri- e   *   **   e- lé- i- son.

(1941).[21] To these titles should be added the monastic editions of the *Antiphonale Monasticum* (1934) and *In nocte Nativitatis Domini ad Matutinum, Missam et Laudes* (1936).

All the chant books cited thus far, except the monastic editions, were published in *editio typica* and in *editio iuxta typicam*. The *editio typica* is the "official" book: almost exclusively published by the *Typis Polyglottis Vaticanis*, and commonly called the *Editio Vaticana*, or simply, the *Vaticana* (VAT). The *editio iuxta typicam* is instead a "private" or "non-official" book, printed by other publishers but in conformity with the *Vaticana* both in regard to the melodies, and in the format and placement of the notes.

The editions of *iuxta typicam* chant published until the Second Vatican Council were those edited by Desclée & Socii. and S. Sedis Apostolicæ et Sacrorum Rituum Congregationis Typographi, and that have added the "rhythmic signs" of Solesmes to the square notation. The frontispiece of every book specifies, "restitutum et editum ad exemplar editionis typicæ concinnatum et rhythmicis signis a Solesmensibus monachis diligenter ornatum,"[22] that is: "restored and published after being arranged according to the model of the *editio typica* and carefully furnished with the rhythmic signs by the monks of Solesmes."

The third phase of the restoration of Gregorian chant is represented by the editions following the liturgical reforms of Vatican II. They are the *Kyriale simplex* (1965), the *Graduale simplex* (in

21. No official edition of the *Liber Responsorialis* has appeared up to the present: neither Dom Mocquereau, who in 1913 was entrusted with the task of continuing the restoration of the books of chant, nor Dom Joseph Gajard, who in 1939 had announced the [forthcoming] complete edition, ever succeeded in bringing the work to completion.

22. The rhythmic signs added to the *editio typica* of the Vatican edition are the *dot* on the right side of a *punctum* and the *horizontal episema* either above or below a note. Beyond these three rhythmic signs, the monks of Solesmes had recourse to two other signs for phrasing: a *tie* or *legatura* between two notes, and the *comma* on the top line of the staff.

1967), the *editio typica* (in 1975), the *editio typica altera*,[23] and the new *Ordo Cantus Missæ* (1972), with the new arrangement of the chants according to the Missal restored by Pope Paul VI.

After the *editio typica altera* of the GS, the *Typis Polyglottis Vaticanis* ceased its activities. The publication of the "official" books of Gregorian chant was entrusted to Solesmes, following the approval of the Congregation for Divine Worship and the Discipline of the Sacraments.

In 1974, the *Graduale Romanum* of 1908 was reprinted, edited by the monks of Solesmes, with the arrangement of the chants conformed to the *Ordo Cantus Missæ* of 1972.[24]

In 1981 the *Psalterium Monasticum* for the ferial office, and in 1983 the *Liber Hymnarius*, were published. With the latter began the publication of the new *Antiphonale Romanum*, on the

23. It is called *altera* (a second one, another one) because this edition introduces the textual version of the Psalms from the New Vulgate (the Gallican psalter, based on the Hebrew text of the Masoretic rabbis.

24. The *Cœtus de libris cantus liturgici revisendis et edendis* (sub-committee for the revision and publication of the books of liturgical chant), presided by Dom E. Cardine, re-ordered, according to the new calendar, the traditional pieces of the *Graduale Romanum*, none of which disappeared: the "treasure" was preserved integrally. Indeed, it was also re-evaluated especially in the Sanctoral, in which all of the pieces of the Neo-Gregorian Masses, centonized at Solesmes beginning a century or so ago, were situated *ad libitum* without mercy and were substituted by chants of the authentic repertory which, up to now, were infrequently sung. The pieces of the Masses suppressed by the reform were in their totality, repositioned elsewhere, sometimes with luck, as for example those of the ferial Masses of the week of Pentecost, obtained, for the most part, from the Discourse after the Last Supper and with the subject of the future works of the Paraclete, that came to form, beginning with the day after the Ascension, a kind of preparatory "novena" to the feast of Pentecost. Also completed was the series of Sundays of the Year, instead of having to repeat during the entire week the *Adorate* Mass, before Lent, and the *Dicit Dominus*, before Advent. For Sundays such as these inedited *Alleluias* were chosen, some of which, drawn from the *Sextuplex* of Dom Hesbert dated back to the best period (Renè-Jean Hesbert, Antiphonale Missarum Sextuplex, Vromant et Cie, Bruxelles [Paris, 1935]). In brief, around twenty chants altogether were recovered, that had fallen into disuse. (J. Claire, "Un secolo di lavoro a Solesmes," *Studi Gregoriani* 16 [2000]: 23).

frontispiece of which is written: "Antiphonale Romanum secundum Liturgiam Horarum ordinemque cantus Officii dispositum a Solesmensibus monachis pracparatum - Tomus alter - Liber Hymnarius." Next to these official editions are those containing the neumatic signs and, anthologies:

The *Graduel Neumé*, 1967, is a reprint of the 1908 edition of the *Graduale Romanum*, with neumes of the school of St. Gall drawn above the square notation by Dom Eugène Cardine, monk of Solesmes and founder of Gregorian semiology.

The *Offertoires Neumés* (or *Triplex*), 1978, is a reprint of the volume first published in 1935 and edited by Karl Ott, containing the Offertory chants of the Roman Gradual with the addition of the melodies of the Offertory verses. The reprint of 1978 contains the neumatic notations of St. Gall, drawn below, and of Metz, drawn above, the square notation by Rupert Fischer, Benedictine monk of Metten.

The *Graduale Triplex*, 1979, is the 1974 edition of the *Graduale Romanum*, with the notation, in black, of the cod. Laon 239 (notation of Metz), added by Marie-Claire Billecocq, the notation, in red, of the cod. St. Gall 359 (*Cantatorium*) for the chants of the soloist, and of cod. Einsiedeln 121 (*Graduale*) for the other chants, added by R. Fischer.

The *Liber Usualis*, various dates of publication, is an "anthological" volume, with extracts from many books, containing chants for the principal feasts of the liturgical year. After the reforms of the Second Vatican Council, the various editions of this book no longer correspond to the new order of the rites, especially that of the Liturgy of the Hours.

The editions that SC had hoped they be realized—"The typical edition of the books of Gregorian chant is to be completed" (117)—and that up till today have yet to be published are the *Antiphonale Romanum* and the *Liber Responsorialis*: with these, the work of the *Consilium ad exsequendam Constitutionem del Sacra Liturgia* could be considered complete. From these two volumes of the *cursus romanus* could be drawn that of the *cursus monasticus*, and, beyond that, the anthological edition of the *Liber Usualis* could be remade.

4. Square-note semiography

The books of chant from the period of the "Vatican" restoration use the square form of the notes that reproduces, in a stylized fashion, the notation of the manuscript sources and the *Corali* of the fifteenth and sixteenth centuries. The choice of the square-note semiography was not motivated by a nostalgic affection for tradition, but rather by the intuition that the graphic placement of the pitches could express a rhythmic significance. For this reason, a search was conducted through the history of graphic evolution, to find that tradition that still presented the square-note shapes, and also respected the graphic groupings of the neumes in *campo aperto*. Notwithstanding imperfections and gaps, this type of semiography resulted in being far superior to every attempt at a transcription using modern notation. The advantages of square notation compared to modern notation are evident for the following reasons: (1) square-note semiography represents a direct evolution from ancient neumatic script; (2) the graphic placement of the neumes in the staff greatly facilitates the perception of the unity of the neume and the design of the melodic movement; (3) the non-mensuralistic form of the notes preserves the concreteness, and at the same time, the indeterminate quality, of their syllabic value; (4) by means of the graphic union or separation of the notes, the square-note form offers the possibility of grasping the unity of, and the various articulations within, the neume, as they are documented in the most ancient manuscripts.[25]

In square-note semiography, the fundamental note is drawn as a *punctum quadratum* (■) that is found isolated on one syllable as well as in composition with other sounds. When it is in composition it can assume the graphic image of a *punctum codatum*,

25. The books of harmonization of Gregorian chants make use of modern notation: in this case the notes used (quarter notes and eighth notes) do not satisfy the same function of expressing a rhythmic fact, as do the neumes. Unfortunately, the transcription into modern notation of the various types of melodic articulation within the poly-group neumes and of the repercussed notes, represent serious difficulties from the point of view of the graphic image.

if it has a stem (¶); in which case, it is called a *virga*, because it represents the highest note.[26]

The *punctum inclinatum*, or diamond shaped (♦), is the element of a descending plurisonic neume whose highest note is written as a *virga*. The graphic image of the *punctum inclinatum* reproduces the movement of a square-tipped pen in the act of writing a series of descending notes. The *punctum dentellatum*, called also the *quilisma* (ᴍ), is a particular graphic image, derived from adiastematic codices, especially those of St. Gall. It expresses a kind of "passing tone," rhythmically very light, and very much joined to the higher sound. The *diminutive liquescent punctum* (♪ | ♩), and the *augmentative liquescent punctum* (♪ | ♪), are graphic images, confirmed in the manuscripts, that indicate the semiological and phonetic phenomenon of *liquescence*, which results from a complex syllabic articulation in the text. The notation of the *liquescent punctum* has undergone a semiographic transformation in the editions of chant beginning with the publication of the AM (1934). The *punctum sinuosum*, also called the *oriscus* (♪), is the neumatic element of melodic tendency, either toward a lower pitch or to a higher pitch, found in many paleographic families. In the books of chant this type of graphic first appeared with the AM; The *punctum stropha* (➤) is a graphic derived from the St. Gall codices that was adopted in the books of chant for the first time in the AM.

5. Complementary elements of square-note semiography

The Staff

The Gregorian melodies are written on a musical staff of four horizontal lines (*tetragram*, from the Greek τετρα, "four," and

---

26. The combination of *virga*, *punctum*, and *virga*, a neume of three notes of which the second is melodically lowest, is reproduced in the current semiography of chant books with the graphic of a thick oblique bar (◣). The first two pitches of the neume are indicated by the position of the beginning and ending points of this oblique bar on the musical staff. This graphic image reconnects with those of the early manuscript sources (∿), that reproduce the movement of the pen drawing the neume without letting the tip of the pen leave the parchment.

γράμμα, "line") with three internal spaces, on which are written the notes that are read from low to high. The lines and spaces, plus the two external spaces, above and below the *tetragram*, form an extension of nine notes, sufficient to contain the greater part of Gregorian melodies. Whenever the chant has a melodic extension such that it is not contained in this space, a change in the position of the clef is used, or ledger lines are added above or below. It is the nearly unanimous opinion that the musical staff originated from the horizontal lines drawn *a secco* to facilitate the calligraphy of the text and the musical notation. It was finalized with the number of four lines in the eleventh century, by Guido d'Arezzo.

Notes

The name of the notes UT, RE, MI, FA, etc. come from the ninth century and were drawn from the first syllables of each line of the first strophe of the Vespers Hymn on the Feast of St. John the Baptist (June 24):

ex. 1.3 LH 382

Ut que- ant la- xis re-so-na-re fi-bris mi- ra ges-tó- rum fá-mu- li

tu- ó- rum, sol- ve pol-lú- ti lá- bi- i re- á- tum, sancte Io- ánnes.

(*So that your servants may, with loosened voices, resound the wonders of your deeds, cleanse the guilt from our stained lips, O St. John.*) [Translation: Margot Fassler, *Music in the Medieval West* 96, W.W. Norton, 2014]

Putting together the first pitch of every incise in the order of their succession creates the hexachordal scale.

ex. 1.4

ut   re   mi   fa   sol   la

The note SI comes from the contraction of the first notes of the last incise "*Sancte Ioannes*." The use of this name, however, comes about only in a later period. Guido, in fact, never uses the name SI, because the semitones within the ancient "empty tone" of the pentatonic scale (B-flat or B-natural) are always named as one of two fixed semitones MI-FA or SI-DO of the natural hexachordal scale UT-LA by means of the system of "mutations" or transpositions, used in the method of solfège. See the example in the following illustration.

ex. 1.5

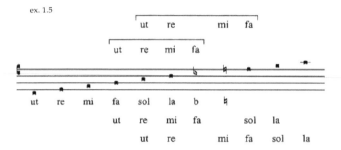

From the eighteenth century the name UT is changed to DO in many areas, possibly in reference to the Italian scholar Giovanni Battista Doni (1594–1647).

Clefs

There are two clefs used in square-note semiography: the DO clef, in the form of a stylized C, and the FA clef in the form of a stylized F.

ex. 1.6

There is a somewhat generic resemblance between the F clefs of the current chant books, and the corresponding letter F. So too for the G clef, that appears a few times in the ancient codices, and for the signs of B-flat and B-natural. The laws of calligraphy after the eleventh century produced in these clefs and signs of alteration such a transformation to render the connection to the alphabetic letters unrecognizable. This is shown in the following table:

ex. 1.7

ETÀ (Century)	CHIAVE di *ut* (C clef)	CHIAVE di *fa* (F clef)	CHIAVE di *sol* (G clef)	B *molle* o *rotundum* (B-flat)	B *durum* o *quadratum* (B-natural)
XI secolo	c	f	G	♭	♮
secoli XII e XIII	c	f f	G	♭	♮
secoli XIV e XV	c	(symbols)	G	♭	♮
Musica moderna	(C clef)	(F clef)	(G clef)	♭	♮

The DO clef is typically found on the third or fourth line of the staff, and occasionally on the second line: cf. *Asperges me*, GR 707, 1–5; Gradual *Laetatus sum*, GR 336,6; Communion. *Passer invenit*, GR 306,5. The FA clef is habitually located on the third line of the tetragram and very rarely on the second; in this position, it is regularly substituted by the DO clef on the fourth line. In one case only, the current chant books use the FA clef on the fourth line: cf. Offertory *Veritas mea*, GR 483,3.

Accidentals

GREG uses only two signs of alteration, the flat and the natural. Limited exclusively to the note B, the ancient "empty note" of the pentatonic system, which became the "movable tone" in the hexachordal system. In Italian, the words used for B-flat and B-natural are, respectively, *bemolle* and *bequadro*. They derive from the letter b: *b-molle*, meaning soft, less tense, and is lowered one half step and drawn with a rounded graphic image ♭; and *b-quadro* (squared), or *b-durum* meaning hard, taut, and is drawn with a squared graphic image ♮.

In the classical repertory the B-flat is placed directly in front of a note within the piece, and it lasts until the change of word, as seen in the following antiphon *exite obviam ei*. The effect of the accidental applies to both B-flat pitches in the word <u>ob-vi-am.</u>

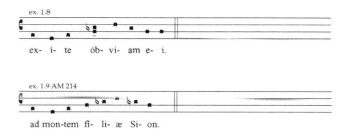

ex. 1.8

ex- i- te   ób- vi- am e- i.

ex. 1.9 AM 214

ad mon-tem fi- li- æ   Si- on.

In the second example, *ad montem filiæ*, the B-flat must be written in the word *filiæ* and again in *Sion* due to the change of word.

ex. 1.10 GR 94

Dó-   mi- ne,

ex. 1.11 GR 476

e-   um.

In the above examples a natural sign is used to cancel the B-flat
before the change of word, and in ex. 1.10 a quarter bar of division.

ex. 1.12 GR 269

[℣. Súscitans]

ex. 1.13 GR 236

Al- le- lu- ia.

In the *Alleluia* example above, the alteration is repeated after the
quarter bar to preserve the B-flat. In the postclassical chants the
B-flat can be found also at the beginning of a piece, immediately
after the clef, with the function of constant alteration: cf. the Marian
antiphons *Alma Redemptoris mater* (AM 173) and *Regina caeli* (AM
176), the antiphons for the Feast of Corpus Christi, *O quam suavis
est* (AM 548) and *O sacrum convivium* (AM 555). There are also

other melodies in which the B-flat, though constant, is repeated continually within the piece: cf. the Marian antiphons *Ave Regina caelorum* (AM 179; GS 475) and *Regina caeli* (AM 179; GS 478).

Guide (custos)

'Ihe *guide* is a sign placed at the end of every line to help the cantor anticipate the position of the first note of the following line of music. This can be found also within the musical staff whenever there is a change of clef.

ex. 1.14 GR 16

Dó-mi- ne.   ℣. Vi- as tu- as:

Bar lines

The bar lines that cut through the staff perpendicularly are lines of punctuation of the melodic-verbal phrasing. There are four types:

1. The double-bar, at the end of a piece or within a piece to mark the alternation between two choirs (cf. the melodies of the Kyriale), or the change of clef;

2. The full-bar, for the subdivision of one part of a melodic-verbal phrase;

3. The half-bar, for the subdivision of a part of a phrase that is melodic-verbal, or only melodic;

4. The quarter-bar, for the subdivision of an incise that is melodic-verbal, or melodic only.

It should be stated immediately that the bar lines of Gregorian semiography have no relation to those of mensural music, and they do not coincide necessarily with rhythmic pauses or vocal breaths. They are, instead, the signs of punctuation of the melodic phrasing, corresponding for the most part to those of a literary text: comma, semicolon, colon, period. VAT proposed these signs of phrasing, inspired by the most recent tradition of the printed sources.

On the actual accuracy, or less, of the bar lines, in relation to the melodic-verbal rhythm, the following can be observed: the double-bar, the full-bar, and the half-bar, in the near totality of cases, give a correct subdivision of both the verbal and the melodic phrasing. In the subdivisions of the incises, on the other hand, that are melodic-verbal, or melodic only, the use of the quarter-bar appears rather subjective: some of them should be corrected, other new ones introduced, and others suppressed. The fundamental criterion for the choice is the text, but not disconnected from criteria of a melodic nature, and similarly, criteria of an aesthetic nature. In the example that follows, the editions of the AM and of the PsM indicate progress with respect to the AR: they maintain the signs of the *episema* for the phrasing of the incises, but remove the quarter-bars in favor of the conceptual unity demanded by the literary text.

ex. 1.15 AR 149

1. In sancti- tá- te   ser-vi- á-mus Dó-mi- no,   et li- be- rá- bit nos

ex. 1.16 AM 65

2. In sancti- tá- te   ser-vi- á-mus Dó-mi- no,   et li- be- rá- bit nos

ex. 1.17 PsM 202

3. In sancti- tá- te   ser-vi- á-mus Dó-mi- no,   et li- be- rá- bit nos

(1) ab in- i- mí- cis nos- tris.

(2) ab in- i- mí- cis nos- tris.

(3) ab in- i- mí- cis nos- tris.

(In holiness and righteousness we might serve him without fear.)
Cf. Luke 1:74-75

In the melodies of the *Sanctus*, VAT almost always uses the quarter-bar after the third *sanctus*, or even the half-bar whenever this word has a semi-ornate or ornate ornamentation such that it expresses a complete formula from the melodic, modal, or rhythmic point of view. In this last case, the use of quarter-bar and even of the half-bar can be justified. In syllabic melodies, however, they are not admissible; in fact, both the textual and the melodic criteria would require that the third *sanctus* not be separated from *Dominus Deus Sabaoth*. And yet, this melodic-verbal context, for example, is observed by VAT in the *Sanctus* XVIII, but not in *Sanctus* XIII.

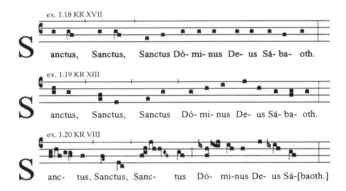

While waiting for a more critical, revised edition of the GR, Solesmes made ample use of two complementary signs in the *Graduale* of 1974: the slur (*legatura*), which appears ninety-two times, and the *comma*, which appears fifty-six times. Firstly, the slur is used to underline the phenomenon of *syneresis* of two neumes on syllables formed by the same vowel (cf. GR 15,4; 275,1); and secondly, to correct the placement of the bar lines, especially when a quarter-bar is placed at the beginning of, or within, a *iubilus*. The *comma* is used to supplement, or to correct, a quarter-bar, for a more exact rhythmic subdivision of the melodic phrasing.

In the example of "*qui te expectant*" (ex. 1.19) from the Introit *Ad te levavi*, the slur was placed to reconstruct the unity of a plurisonic neume that in VAT was written in a *dieresis* version in relation to the number of the syllables. In the next example, the *iubilus*[27] of the final syllable of "*Domi-ne*" (from the Gr. *Universi*),

27. In the GR of 1908, the slur is used only once in relation to melodic phrasing, correcting a full bar: cf. In. *Suscepimus Deus* (GR 300,7 and 543,6). In the GR of 1974, the slur is used frequently to indicate a melodic-verbal phrasing, correcting, most of the time, a quarter bar (GR 46,5; 47,1; 74,8; 83,2; 133,1; 159,3; 205,1; 283,2; 303,2; 322,3; 338,8; 440,4; 464,3), but sometimes a half bar (GR 366,2; 573,2) and even a full bar (GR 27,2; 404,8; 500,5; 568,4). The slur is used to correct the quarter bar at the beginning of a *iubilus* (GR 16,2; 19,7; 112,7; 121,2; 151,3; 206,8; 223,6; 282,8; 337,2), or within the *iubilus* (GR 207,1–2; 258,4–5; 299,3; 322,2; 459,1). In the GT of 1979, Solesmes extended the use of the slur, always to correct a quarter bar within a *iubilus,* in the *responsum* of the Graduals of Mode II in A (GR 25,4; 27,7; 30,5). In many other cases it would have been necessary to intervene, providing an important service to those who need a guide to understanding the articulations of melodic phrasing.

having been interrupted by the quarter-bar immediately after the generating note of the neume, is then reconstructed in its unity by the slur.

In the example *Reminiscere* (1.12 above), the *comma* was drawn to correct the two quarter-bars of VAT and to indicate the exact placement of the punctuation of the phrase member.[28] Specifically, VAT placed two quarter-bars, one after the word *Reminiscere*, and one after *tuarum*, corresponding to the textual comma. The incise-word *Domine* consists of a semi-ornate redundant cadential formula. There was no need to separate with a quarter-bar what is only a redundant cadence. It was probably done for the fact that this cadence is a prolongation, similar to a "codetta," using the redundant formula on MI of "*tuarum*." The quarter-bar after the verb *Reminiscere* is superfluous, then, and risky for the interpretation. It is certain that here too the quarter-bar was placed to correspond to the asterisk of the text, which indicated the end point of the cantor's intonation. Instead, the true melodic articulation of the phrase comes at the final syllable of "*miseratio-num*," precisely where Solesmes placed the *comma*. A breath is indicated at this exact point between the two equivalent melodic-verbal units, represented by *miserationum* and by *tuarum*, that begin with the same neume and add up to an equal number of notes.

To pretend to give meticulous and quantitatively detailed indications on how to perform the phraseological punctuations of the bar lines is useless and misleading. Nor can a hierarchy of pauses and rests be established for the various signs of punctuation of the literary text. It would be a mistake to do so! The same can be said for the verbal-melodic punctuation as well as for the

---

28. The *comma* has the function of a "melodic articulation," the same way as a quarter bar. It is used on the basis of three criteria: (1) to compensate for the lack of a sign of melodic articulation (GR 62,2); (2) to correct a nearby bar line, shifting the articulation to the correct place of the melody (GR 404,8); (3) to highlight a significant verbal articulation (GR 98,7) or avoid an undue blending of melodic elements (GR 27,5; 332,6).

melodic ones. The bar lines are signs of punctuation that become concrete in a specific context. In Gregorian chant, an obligatory metronomic time does not exist. Rather, there are syllabic values and groupings to be actuated. It is not the bar lines that are to be interpreted, but the qualities of the various phraseological units. A proportionate "natural breath" of the melody cannot be ignored at the larger bar lines, such as the half or the whole bar. This is all the more so given that Gregorian is, above all, vocal melody. As can already be inferred, mature discussion on interpretation calls for the assimilation of many aspects of Gregorian chant study.

Asterisk (*)

The asterisk is the punctuation sign of the mediant cadence (*mediatio*) in the psalm tones, whereas in the chants of the Mass and of the Office, it is the sign of division between the intonation of the soloist and the entrance of the choir. The GR of 1974 removed the asterisk from the end of the *versus* of the Gradual, of the Alleluia, and of the last *versus* of the Tract.[29] At the ninth invocation

---

29. In the *Praenotanda* (GT 10) it is stated: "After the first reading the *Responsorium Graduale* is performed by the cantors or by the choir. Then, the *versus* is performed through to the end by the cantors. Hence, there is no reason for inserting an asterisk to indicate a resumption of the singing by the choir at the end of the Gradual versicle, or the Alleluia, or the last verse of the Tract. When it seems opportune, the first part of the responsory may be repeated, as far as the versicle." ("Post primam lectionem dicitur Responsorium Graduale a cantoribus vel a choro. Versus autem a cantoribus profertur usque ad finem. Nulla proinde ratio habenda est asterisci, quo indicatur resumptio cantus a choro facienda in fine versus Gradualis, versus ad Alleluia et ultimi versus Tractus. Quando autem opportunum videtur, licet repetere primam partem Responsorii usque ad versus") (n. 5). Regarding the performance practice of the *Alleluia*, the *Prænotanda* states: "The *Alleluia*, with its melisma (*iubilus*), is sung through by the cantors and then repeated by the choir. However, if necessary, it may be sung only once by all. The versicle is performed in its entirety by the cantors, after which the *Alleluia* is repeated by all." ("Alleluia cum suo neumate canitur totum a cantoribus et repetitur a choro. Pro opportunitate tamen cantari potest semel tantum ab omnibus. Versus a cantoribus profertur usque in finem; post ipsum vero Alleluia ab omnibus repetitur") (n. 7).

of a melodically ornate *Kyrie*, the single asterisk indicates the point of alternation of the choirs, and the double asterisk indicates the singing of the choirs together. This, however, is not an obligatory performance practice.

Cross (✝)

The cross is the punctuation sign for the *flex*, indicating a textual caesura. It is used during the chanting of the Psalms in the Divine Office when the first part of a psalm verse has a long text.

CHAPTER 2

THE TEXT[1]

Introduction

Gregorian chant can be compared to an opera libretto placed in the hands of a composer to be translated into music. This libretto has texts of various genres, grouped according to literary style (prose or poetry), liturgical season (Advent, Christmas, Lent, Easter, Ordinary Time, Sanctoral Cycle), theme (prayers of supplication, of thanksgiving, for mercy or pardon, etc.) and origins (Psalter, other Sacred Scripture, hagiography). The literary construction (syllable, word, phrase) represents the material aspect (body), whereas the thematic content in its liturgical context, represents the spiritual aspect (soul). From these two elements, inseparably united, flows the textual rhythm, which, in turn, becomes the foundation of a melodic rhythm, insofar as the melody is placed at the service of the qualities of the text and, at the same time, transfigures them and renders them sublime.

It is fundamentally important, therefore, to give careful attention to the proclamation of the text. This includes the correct declamation

1. The author acknowledges the contribution of Rev. Maurus Mount, OSB, PhD, who reviewed the translations of Latin quotations from the Roman Grammarians in this chapter.

and accentuation of the syllables of a word, and a proper search for the phrasing, that is, the grouping of the smaller rhythmic entities made by the words, with the necessary distinctions between the phrase members, and between the phrases themselves. The elements that combine to form a literary text are the syllable, the word, and the groups of words; from these take shape the incise, the phrase member, and the phrase.

1. The syllable

The syllable (from the Greek συλλαβη, "a group of letters"), is the phonetic unit of language and the constitutive element of a word, whose sound is pronounced with a single emission of the voice. A syllable is graphically represented by one, or more, letters, at least one of which is a vowel. The vowels are the sonorous part of a text, and, as such, can form syllables by themselves. The consonants, on the other hand, do not resonate unless united to vowels.

The phenomenon that determines the solvency[2] of the resonance when passing from syllable to syllable is commonly called "syllabic articulation." This articulation can be of the vocalic type if the solvency occurs between two vowels (*De-us me-us*), of a consonantal type if the solvency is between vowels and consonants (*Do-mi-nus, di-co vo-bis*). In these, the solvency can be more or less resonant. The phonetic phenomenon of liquescence, caused mainly by the encounter of two consonants, or by the presence of a diphthong, holds back the fluidity of the articulation and produces a significant sonority: *ad-ver-sum me, non con-fun-den-tur*. In other cases, though, this kind of resonance is barely noticeable: *ad-o-ra-te Do-mi-num*.

From the phonetic point of view, every vowel and consonant must correspond to a particular position of the oral cavity, to avoid the defect of giving each syllable the same color. In a more or less

---

2. The Latin root of "solvency," *solvo, solvere, solvi, solutus*, translates as: to loosen, release, unbind, etc. English derivatives include: *solve, solvent, solution, resolve, absolve, dissolve.*

rapid succession of syllables, it is necessary to change the position of the vocal organs with a corresponding agility. A fundamental presupposition for the interpretation of Gregorian chant is this particular attention to vocalic diction.

The relationship of the various idioms with the Latin language can facilitate, more or less, the correct diction of the Latin text. Certain defects, however, should be avoided: for instance, pronouncing a semi-mute *e* at the end of words that end in consonants; uniting in a kind of diphthong the final two syllables of a proparoxytonic word (*iustí-tia*); contracting words to negate the hiatus ("*Teternum*" instead of *Te æternum*), mispronouncing the double consonants ("*aleluia*" or "*qui tollis*" instead of *aleluia* and *qui tollis*).

The following syllabic particularities, commonly overlooked, should be noted:

1. The letter *i*, preceded by or followed by a vowel, does not form a diphthong (*pro-ge-ni-e, fi-li-us, Spi-ri-tu-i, in-tro-i-bo*), unless it derives from the letter *j*, in which case it forms not an autonomous vowel, but a diphthong with the vowel that follows it (*e-ius, al-le-lu-ia, Ia-cob*). In these cases, the sonority is actuated on the second vowel, contrary to what happens on all other diphthongs:

℞. Gau- dé- te ius- ti

In the word *eleison* of the Kyrie, VAT separates the two vowels of the diphthong *ei*, obtaining a proparoxytone of four syllables (*e-le-i-son*), rather than a paroxytone of three syllables with a liquescent between the accent and the final (*e-lei-son*). The solution of the VAT may not be the best when considered in the light of the paleographic evidence that reserves for this word the same treatment as for a liquescent paroxytone (*ex-cél-sis*), as can be seen in the following examples.[3]

---

3. E. Cardine, "Esthétique du mot eleison," *Revue Grégorienne* 37 (1958): 127.

ex. 2.2.

In this regard, Dom Mocquereau, in his article on Kyrie X, wrote: "The monks of Solesmes would have written—in the projected Kyriale presented to the first Vatican Commission of 1905— the syllable "lei" as a diphthong:

in accordance with the manuscripts, in which the agreement is nearly unanimous in making "eleison" a three-syllable word. This tradition has been preserved very faithfully, especially in the German lands, wherein the formerly official Regensburg edition it is never written in any other way."[4]

2. The letter *u*, preceded by the vowel *a* usually forms a diphthong (*gáu-di-um, ex-áu-di*); but does not form a diphthong when followed by a vowel (*tu-um, retribu-e, meru-i*). The union of letters *e* and *u* (*eu*) is a diphthong (*eu-ge*) except when the *u* creates a syllable with a consonant (*De-us*).

3. The combinations *qu* and *gu* form diphthongs with the following vowels: *quém, relínquo, pinguédine*. On the contrary, in the verb *árguas* it is not a diphthong because the word derives from the verb *ar-gú-e-re* where the vowel u, carrying the accent, determines the *dieresis* of the diphthong. The combination *ph* is pronounced *f*, and the words *nihil* and *mihi* are pronounced as they appear in the Gregorian codices: *nichil* and *michi*.[5] The unaccented group *ti*, when followed by a vowel, is usually pronounced *tsi* (*ju-stí-ti-a, pá-ti-ens, o-ti-ó-sus, ó-ti-um*). However, it preserves the sound of *t* when preceded by another *t*, by *s*, or by *x* (*Cót-tius, vés-ti-o,*

4. "Les moines de Solesmes avaient écrit [dans le projet de Kyriale présenté en 1905 à la première Commission vaticane] la syllabe *lei* en diphtongue: conformément aux manuscrits dont l'accord est presque unanime pour faire du mot *eleison* un trisyllabe. Cette tradition s'était conservée assez fidèlement, surtout dans les pays allemands, pour que l'édition de Ratisbonne, jadis officielle, n'écrivît pas différemment." "The monks of Solesmes had written the syllable *lei* as a diptong, in accordance with the manuscripts that are almost unanimous in considering the word *eleison* as trisyllabic. This tradition had been followed sufficiently strictly, in particular in the German countries, for the Ratisbonne edition, formerly the offical one, not to write it differently." Cf. Dom Mocquereau and Dom Beyssac, "Kyrie: Alme Pater," *Rassegna gregoriana* (1907): 293–294, n. 1.

5. The insertion of the letter *c* before the *h*, both in the personal pronoun *michi* and in the word *nichil*, is due to the intentional choice of the monastic scribecantors to reinforce the consonantic value as an aspirated vowel that it had lost since the imperial period (second century).

míx-ti-o (pronounced "*mic-sti-o*") or when the *i* falls on the accent: *pe-tí-e-rant, to-tí-us).*[6]

4. When a vowel is repeated it forms two distinct syllables (*mánu-um, su-um*). When spoken in an oratorical rhythm it is generally better to separate them (*Si iniquitates, qui te expectant, mortu-us, mi-hi in Domino*). When they are sung, however, it is preferable to pronounce a single vowel, maintaining the syllabic value of the notes that ornament both vowels. This interpretation is supported by some of the most trustworthy manuscript sources that use a single plurisonic neume in these contexts, that is, where there is a repetition of the same vowel. In the GR of 1908 and in the successive editions up until 1974, VAT prefers the criteria of other manuscript sources that attribute a separate neume to each vowel. The 1974 edition of the GR prefers the criteria of a single neume in non-cadential melodic contexts: the square-note semiography of the preceding editions should be corrected by uniting the neumes of the two equal vowels with a slur. An example of this can be found in the In. *Ad te levavi*, at the words *qui te expectant* (p. 213 ex. A.1). In these cases the performance of a single neume demands a typographical change in the text also; for instance, writing the neume on the second vowel while writing the first vowel in italics, as was the common practice when writing the extra syllable in the verses of the Hymns.

ex. 2.4. GR 15

ét- e- nim u- ni- vér- si qui teex- spéc- tant,

The same criteria is applied to the melodies of the *Kyrie*. Only the first *e* vowel of the first syllable of eleison is to be sung, and not

---

6. It is preferable to maintain the sound *t* when the unaccented syllable *ti* is followed by another *i*, to avoid losing the phonetic quality of the ending represented by the second *i* (*pe-ti-i*), although from the point of view of the Latin form, it would be more correct to pronounce the *t* as a *z*.

the final syllable of *Kyrie* or of *Christe*, and regarding the typography, the latter *e* should be written in italics: (Ky-ri-*e* e-lei-son, Chris-t*e* eleison).

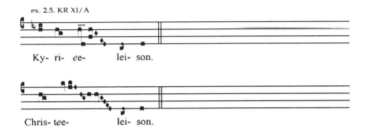

ex. 2.5. KR XI/A

Ky- ri- ee-   lei- son.

Chris- tee-   lei- son.

2. The single word

A word is formed by the coming together of syllables. These represent, however, only the material and formless portion of the word. That which gives *soul*, *life*, and *unity* to a word is the *accentuation*, from which flow the qualities of melody, tone color, and the rhythm of the word. Accentuation does not identify with verbal accents but is rather a melodic-rhythmic phenomenon that contextually embraces the entire word. The ancient grammarians used the terminology *accentus acutus* (acute syllable) to define the accented syllable of the word, and the terminology of "*accentus*" by itself to define the accentuation, understood as *anima* and *forma* of the entire word.

3. Latin accentuation

In order for the accentuation to express the unity of the word, the accent syllable must be correctly placed with regard to its *tendency toward*, and its *dying onto*, the final syllable. When the accent syllable is the pole of animation and cohesion of the syllables that precede the final, impressing upon them a melodic movement that is balanced and fluid with respect to their innate phonic qualities, it is placed correctly. Since these qualities of the Latin language have not remained unchanged over the centuries, it is essential to examine the character of the Latin grammatical accent at the period of the major production or, at the very least, of the primitive sources of the liturgical chant of the Church of Rome.

A. During the Classical Period (second century BC–fourth century AD) the Latin accent is melodic, and for this reason is called the tonic accent, or simply, *tone*. In the declamation of a text, every syllable has a specific intonation proper to it: the accent syllable has the most acute melodic intonation with respect to the other syllables.

"The nature of prosody consists in the fact that acute accents alternate with grave accents. In fact, the acute sound is so clearly perceptible that if all the syllables were pronounced at the same pitch there would be no prosody. . . . The accent *determines the pitch*; when a part of a word is lowered towards a grave pitch or is raised to an acute pitch. . . ."[7]

B. "One might say that nature itself had intentionally arranged to modulate the human voice, placing in every word an acute accent, and not more than one, and never before the antepenultimate syllable"[8] (M. T. Cicero, 106–43 BC).

Furthermore, this is placed on the vowel of the penultimate syllable if that syllable is long, or on the vowel of the syllable which is third from the end, if the penultimate is short; never at the end of a word, nor beyond the third syllable from the end.[9]

---

7. "Natura vero prosodiæ in eo est quo taut sursum est aut decorsum; nam in vocis altitudine omnino spectator, adeo ut, si omnes syllabæ pari fastigio vocis enuntientur, prosodia sit nulla. . . . Ab altitudine discernit accentus, cum pars verbi aut in grave deprimitur aut sublimatur in acutum." *Sergium, De accentibus* (*GL* IV. p. 525, 18). Attributed to Varro. See G. Goetz and F. Schoell, *F. M. Terenti Varronis De lingua latina quae supersunt* (Leipzig: Teubner, 1910), 213.

8. "Ipsa enim natura quasi modularetur hominum orationem, in omni verbo posuit acutum vocem nec una plus nec a postrema sillaba citra tertiam." Cf. M. T. Cicero (106–43 BC) *De orat.* XVIII, 58.

9. The words which have their own connotation contain one accent syllable, including monosyllables. Consequently, the following have no accent: (1) the enclitics (*que, ve, ne, nam*) and (2) the monosyllabic additions (*ce, pse, dem, met*) that rely on the previous word (*multáque, itáque,* or *ítaque*—the first stands for

"Accents are determined from the last syllables, not from the first; that is, in reverse, nor can they move back, except as far as the third syllable from the end."[10]

In the postclassical period of Latin (end of fourth century–end of fifth century AD), the musical and melodic character of the accent remains, but, gradually the qualities of intensity and strength are added to it. With regard to the position of the accent in the word, there are no substantial differences with the classical period. A word with two syllables carries the accent on the first syllable and is called a paroxytone or tonic *spondee*; a word with three syllables carries the accent on the first syllable if the penultimate is considered brief in the classical period and is called a proparoxytone or a tonic *dactyl*; finally, a one-syllable word, with a tonic accent (*laus, cor, rex*) is called an *oxytone*.

C. Another characteristic of the grammatical accent is *brevity*. The element of quantity—long and short syllables—in classical Latin prosody diminishes, and all the syllables are more or less brief. Thus, in words with more than three syllables, next to the intense melodic accent, a secondary accent, also called a counter-

---

et ita with an exhortative meaning, "and so"; and the second, with a conclusive meaning, "therefore"; given the substantive similarity of the two meanings and the difficulty of grasping their distinction, it is preferable to always pronounce it the second way: *ítaque*): *hódiéque, vidésne, magis minúsve, útinam, illiúsce, reápse, ibídem, égomet,* i*psemet*; (3) the preposition *cum* added to a pronoun: *vobíscum, nobíscum, técum*; (4) the conjunctions (*et, sed, atque, sicut, quia*) when placed at the head of the sentence or phrase (*sicut erat, quia fecit mihi magna*), unless they are isolated from what follows, forming an ellipsis: *Et: Tu in princípio, Domine; Non dixit, Iesus, non moritur, sed: sic eum volo manére*; (5) prepositions and adverb-prepositions, when they are prepended to the word (*de profúndis, in ætérnum, super vos, per ómnia, post partum, ante oculos*; (6) relative pronouns, when there is the antecedent to which they refer (*Deus qui fecit*). With Greek and Hebrew words the accent is adopted in the Latin manner on the penultimate (*Dávid, Iácob*) or on the third to last syllable (*Melchísedech, Móyses*).

10. "Accentus autem computantur non a prioribus syllabis, sed ab ultimis, id est retrorsum, nec possunt ascendere nisi usque ad tertiam syllabam a fine." Cf. M. Servius (fourth century AD), in *Donatum, De accentibus* (GL, IV, fasc. II, p. 426, 20).

accent, begins to appear. It is placed on alternate syllables beginning from the principal accent.

Concretely, the syllables that can receive a secondary accent are: (1) the pre-tonic syllables (*mú-li-é-ri-bus, mi-sé-ri-cór-di-a, trí-bu-lá-ti-ó-nes*), (2) the final syllables of proparoxytones, and (3) the monosyllables when there are more than three syllables between the two principal accents (*gáu-di-úm os nóstrum, Dó-mi-nús ex Síon, ómnia quæ' movéntur, manet ín ætérnum*). The existence of the secondary accent is documented in metric poetry, based, essentially, on binary rhythm/accentuation. For example:

Líber scríptus próferétur,	The written book will be brought forth,
ín quo tótum cóntinétur	in which all is contained,
únde múndus iúdicétur.	from which the world shall be judged.

(from the sequence *Dies iræ*, LH 127; translation from *St. Andrew Daily Missal* [St. Paul, MN: E. M. Lohmann, 1962], p. 1582)

Nítet véstra dómus	Your house shines
flóribús virtútum,	and with every beautiful virtue,
únde grátiárum	the source of grace
fóns prománat ípse.	perennially flows.

(from the hymn *Christe splendor Patris*, LH 29; translation by Fr. Dylan Schrader in *Hymnal for the Hours*, Rev. Samuel F. Weber, OSB [2014])

It is documented elsewhere in the Gregorian melody, and, above all, in psalmody, where some cadences—for instance, those of two accents—require the use of a secondary accent.

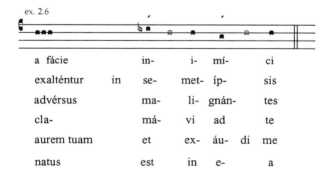

ex. 2.6

a fácie		in-	i-	mí-		ci
exalténtur	in	se-	met-	íp-		sis
advérsus		ma-	li-	gnán-		tes
cla-		má-	vi	ad		te
aurem tuam		et	ex-	áu-	di	me
natus		est	in	e-		a

D. The melodic and intense character of the accent, together with the literary construction of the Latin texts without quantitative prosody (that is, with brief syllables), basically coincides with the most significant musical production (that is, the primitive sources) of the Church of Rome. For this reason the postclassical period of Latin is commonly called the Ecclesiastical Period of Latin. The graphic signs of Latin accentuation also received detailed descriptions on the part of the ancient grammarians. The syllable of the melodically elevated intonation is distinguished by the graphic sign of the acute accent (ὀξεῖα προσῳδία). Due to its importance it is also called κύριος τόνος (principal tone, authoritative, Lord). It is drawn from low to high, from left to right. The final syllable, on the contrary, is distinguished by the grave accent (βαρεῖα προσῳδία) because, just like a verbal cadence that descends melodically, it is pronounced with a lower tone of voice. The first pre-tonic syllable (*mi-se-ri-córdia*) is equivalent to the final. Varro writes: "The acute note is represented by a dash drawn upwards from left to right, and the grave by a similar dash with the lower stroke on the same part (that is, from left to right). These signs demonstrate that every acute syllable is higher and that every grave syllable is lower."[11]

The graphic signs of these two accents represent a musicological fact of extreme importance regarding the origins of the paleographic musical notation of Gregorian chant.[12]

The atonic syllables, or unstressed syllables, that precede or follow the tonic accent of a polysyllabic word (*dilexísti*, *necessitátibus*), receive a medium accent. They are pronounced in melodic

---

11. "Acutæ nota est virgule a sinistra parte dextrorsum sublimæ fastigata / ; gravis autem notatur simili virgule ab eadem parte depresso fastigio / , quæ notæ demonstrant omnem acutam vocem sursum esse et gravem deorsum." Cf. Varro, *apud Servium, De accentibus* (GL IV, fasc. II, 27).

12. Two other accents were used by grammarians for the prosodically long syllables: the *circumflex* accent (^), which has its origins in the combination of the acute accent with the grave accent, used for accent syllables; and the *inverted circumflex*, originating in the combination of the grave accent with the acute accent, for the final syllables.

progression, ascending and descending, depending on whether they move toward the principal accent or towards the final syllable.

By alternating "melodically" between tonic and grave syllables, a particular musical language emerges, in which the ancients recognized a kind of *embryonic* melody: "Even in spoken language, after all, there is a kind of song, only a little less so";[13] and "The accent, as some have claimed, is the soul of the word and the beginning of music, since every melody is composed of acute and grave accents, therefore the accent was considered 'close to song' (*accentus/adcantus*)."[14]

It should be noted, however, that the phonetic characteristic of the Latin language was not to be reduced to precise and absolute melodic intervals. They were rather minimal, or nearly enharmonic, and varied according to the vocal capacity or the psychological state of the one who pronounced them.

Of the two general signs for the accents and the others derived from them, the circumflex and the inverted circumflex, only the sign of the acute accent remains in use, the progressive evolution of the Latin language gradually abandoning the others.

Though drawn in broad strokes, this *excursus* on the nature of the Latin text's grammatical accents and the phenomenon of accentuation permit the formulation of some significant conclusions:

1. The melodic, intense, and brief character of the accent syllable found abundant application in the melodies of Gregorian chant. This can be verified in the examples on pp. 90–106.

2. The phenomenon of Latin accentuation is the basis of Gregorian rhythmic interpretation. Melodic-verbal unity flows from the relationship between the poles of animation (arsis), represented

---

13. "Est autem etiam in dicendo quidam cantus obscurior." Cf. M. T. Cicero, *Orat.* XVIII, 57.

14. "Et est accentus, ut quidam putaverunt, anima vocis et seminarium musices, quod omnis modulatio ex fastigiis vocum gravitateque componitur ideoque accentus quasi adcantus dictus est." Cf. M. Capella (early fifth–sixth century AD), *De nuptiis, lib. III, de arte grammatica* (F. Eyssenhardt, *Martianus Capella* [Leipzig: Teubner, 1866], p. 65, 19).

by the syllables that receive order and cohesion around the accent, and the pole of relaxation (thesis), represented by the final syllable.

3. The graphic signs of the accents from Latin grammar become the general and universal signs for the emerging notation of chant: the acute accent takes the name *virga*, the grave accent the name *punctum*; the circumflex accent, derived from the combination of acute accent with the grave accent, takes the name *clivis*, and the inverted circumflex accent, derived from the combination of the grave accent with the acute, the name *pes*, or *podatus*.

4. Rhythm

Within the context of a word, syllables play a more or less important role. The rhythmic accentuation unites and fuses the syllables together according to their quality, giving them a melodic character intoned in the shape of a melodic arc. The appropriate manner of declaiming the syllables, passing from one syllable to the next, is called *syllabic articulation*. Syllabic articulations evolve around two fundamental poles: the pole of the accent, also called pole of animation or of tension (*arsis*), and the pole of the final, also called pole of relaxation (*thesis*). The pole of animation has its focal point around the accented syllable, which attracts the preceding syllable(s) to itself and transmits that momentum through the following syllable(s) to the pole of relaxation, the final syllable. Rhythm uses these two poles to impart unity, autonomy, and clarity to the words and phrases.

Monosyllabic words with their own accent, except when they are the final word of a phrase, are considered a pole of animation, toward which the verbal rhythm converges, without change to what precedes or follows. They should not be treated as enclitic syllables: *Salvum mé fác Deus; nisi tú, Deus noster; és tú*—not *és tu*, nor *es tú*.

In the pole of animation the accent is understood and interpreted as a vital element (*anima vocis*) but not as an intensive impulse or longer in duration. On the other hand, the final syllable represents (except in rare exceptions such as *factus est*) the pole of relaxation within the word. It gives a sense of completion to the word, in its rhythm, in its unity, and in its meaning. Ignoring this value in the final syllable will collapse the correct syllabic articulation, and might result in the following crude and strange creations:

"Patriet"	instead of	*Patri et (Filio)*
"Paxominibus"	instead of	*pax hominibus*
"Sedea"	instead of	*sede a (dextris)*
"Accipécoronam"	instead of	*accipe coronam*
"Spiritútuo"	instead of	*spiritu tuo*

Misrepresentations of this kind are more likely to happen in the Hymns, where the melody is always the same for every strophe, for instance in the hymn *Pange lingua*, on the phrase "*comparsit laudatio*" instead of *compar sit laudatio*.

On the final syllable the voice should fall naturally, without diminishing its value or duration, so as to highlight the distinctions and divisions of the different words.

Any pre-tonic or intermediary post-tonic syllables are understood in reference to the accents and to the fundamental syllabic articulations of the final syllables. On these secondary articulations the voice should avoid the extremes of giving them unnecessary weight, or of rushing them and colliding with the principal articulation. In words such as *misericórdia, iustítia*, and *spirítuum*, every syllable should preserve its autonomy in the context of the unity of the word moving toward the final.

Obviously, some syllables will have more weight with respect to others, because they contain more consonants. But even in these cases, the differentiation of the syllabic values should not change their quality and function in the context of the unity of the word. In concrete terms, every word should begin with a movement that converges toward the accent syllable and from there pass to the final syllable. Only in this way will a legato verbal style emerge, understood as a union of syllables. To the contrary, blocking the rhythmic flow on a random syllable, or giving an impulse where it does not belong, destroys the unity of the word, and results in a "spelling out" of a word, rather than a natural "speaking" of the word. In the same way, an intense exaggeration of the tonic accent will render unintelligible the other syllables. It is all about the correct realization of the verbal articulation, which has its solvency in the pole of animation (the accent syllable) and its dissolvency in the pole of relaxation (final syllable), where the verbal unity and autonomy is actuated.

5. The "expanded" word

In literary texts single words do not have absolute autonomy but are united in groups of two or more words in relation to the conceptual meaning they are called upon to express. The connection between words comes about through the *verbal articulation* (sometimes called *conclusive syllabic articulation*) that happens in the passage from the final syllable of one word to the first syllable of the next.

Therefore, in the same way that a word has *syllabic articulations*, the subdivisions of phrasing (incises, phrase members, phrases) originate in *verbal articulations*. When written, these phraseological subdivisions are made visible by punctuation marks (comma, colon, semi-colon), while in spoken language they are made audible by pauses or other vocal interruptions. To arrive at a correct phrasing of a text, it is necessary to know its literary construction and its meaning.

The *incise* is the most simple proposition in the context of a *phrase*; it is based on conceptual unity and on the function of certain verbal entities. The *phrase member* is a larger subdivision than the incise, with a more or less complete meaning in the context of a phrase. Finally, the phrase is one or more propositions (incises or phrase members) with complete meaning.

	phrase		
		phrase member	
		incises	
Proprio Filio suo	*non pepér-cit Deus,*	*sed pro nobis omnibus*	*tradidit illum.*
(His own Son	God did not spare,	but for us all	he delivered him up.)

If the phrasing of the incises breaks the conceptual unity, strange and incorrect expressions might result, for example:

sed pro nobis / omnibus *tradidit illum* (but for us / all delivered him up)	instead of	*sed pro nobis omnibus /* *tradidit illum.* (but for us all / he deliv- ered him up)
ad dandam scientiam / *salutis plebi eius* (to give knowledge [and] salvation to his people)	instead of	*ad dandam scientiam sa-* *lutis / plebi eius* (to give knowledge of sal- vation / to his people)
et Iesum benedictum / *fructum ventris tui* (and Jesus blessed / the fruit of thy womb)	instead of	*et Iesum / benedictum* *fructum ventris tui* (and Jesus / the blessed fruit of thy womb)

Large or small, every oratorical phrase is an arch form of three phases:

1. The *apex*: the phase of the high point of the oratorical arch where the principal phrase accent resides

2. The *antecedent*: the phase of preparation for the apex, or, the phase of elevation

3. The *consequent*: the phase of repose, relaxation, or, the phase of descent toward the final[15]

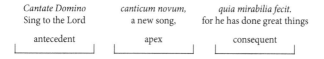

Cantate Domino	*canticum novum,*	*quia mirabilia fecit.*
Sing to the Lord	a new song,	for he has done great things
antecedent	apex	consequent

15. Dom Mocquereau subdivides the arch construction of the melodic phrase into *protasis*, the first part that includes the apex, and *apodasis*, the second part of the phrase, from the apex to the end (cf. *Le nombre musical grégorien, ou, rythmique grégorienne, théorie et pratique*, vol. 2, [Rome and Tournai: Desclée & Cie, 1927], 564). In the larger melodic phrases, the two parts are again subdivided into *incisi/protasis* and into *incisi/apodosis*.

This literary arch construction is realized not only in the phrase, but also within the phrase members, within an incise, and even within the rhythmic unit of a word. In the latter, the phrasing is identified with the rhythm and the verbal articulation.

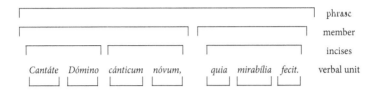

In every word, the apex coincides with the tonic accent; the antecedent phase corresponds to the pre-tonic syllables; and the consequent phase to the post-tonic syllables and/or the final syllable. Monosyllabic words are joined to form words, or pseudo-words, of two or three syllables. In many cases the oratorical apex is not placed in a symmetrical way at the center of a phrase because the antecedent is preceded by another phrase member that can be identified as a *prosthesis* (from the Greek προσθεσις, "addition").

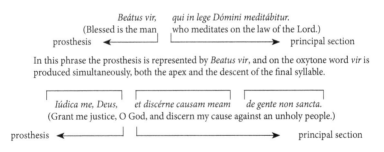

In the second example above, the principal phrase has its apex on the pronoun *meam*. The antecedent (*et discerne causam meam*) is preceded by a prosthesis in which an arch construction can once again be seen.

It is important to grasp the meaning of a literary text so as to give to each of its parts a correct and harmonious place in the phrasing, since it is always a free (prose) rhythm and phrasing and not a measured (metric) one, based on the phrasing of discourse and literary language, and not on strict and immutable laws. The first real pause in a literary piece would come at the conclusion of a phrase member, and the second pause at the end of a phrase; the latter being longer than the former since it serves not only to conclude the whole phrase but also to separate it from the following phrase.

In the following pages it will be interesting to verify how the melodic ornamentation and the aesthetic-modal construction recognizes these textual aspects.

CHAPTER 3

MELODY (Part I)

1. *Legato* melodic-verbal style

In Gregorian chant, the qualities of the literary text move in *symbiosis* with those of the melody. Syllables come together to form words, and words to form literary phrases. Analogously, *syllable-neumes* form *text-melodies*, and these combine to form melodic phrases. The principal parts of a *text-melody* are the *accent syllable-neume* and the *final syllable-neume*. The former is the pole of animation, lift, or *arsis*; the latter is the pole of relaxation, repose, or *thesis*. These two poles are complementary: they depend not only on the sense of unity and meaning within the word but also on the melodic ornamentation that the composer has given them. Together the two poles impart order and cohesion to the rhythmic synthesis of the phenomenon of *Latin accentuation*.

The introduction of this volume mentioned the melodic genres with which Gregorian monody has ornamented the ritual Word: syllabic, semi-ornate, and ornate, or melismatic. The ornate genre is characterized by neumes which are melodically very prolonged, even to the point of being true melodies[1] in their own right. These melodies are formed of neumatic groupings, aesthetically ordered according to the mode of the piece, each of which reproducing,

---

1. From the Greek μελος (song), that is, a succession of modulated sounds that form, to be precise, a song.

so to speak, a unity similar to the text-melody, but established instead as a *word-melody*. This process is clearly seen in the many tropes[2] composed on the melismas of the *Alleluia*, as shown in the following example.

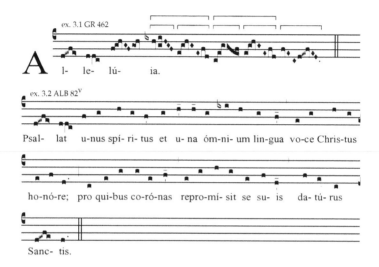

In the ornate genre, the Gregorian composer *expands* the word of the text, not by repeating it, but by substituting the syllables of a text with the articulations within the neumatic groups that form the melody. The ornate genre represents the culmination, after the syllabic and semi-ornate genres, of the literary text's sublimation: from the literary word takes shape the text-melody, and from this derives a *word-melody*.

2. The accent syllable-neume

The accent syllable-neume is, in general, more elevated melodically than the neumes on the other syllables, and this underscores

---

2. From the Greek τρόπος (mode, method), from which derives "troping," the method of applying a text to pre-existing melismas.

its role as the pole of animation. The Latin accent and the melodic apex frequently coincide, especially in the psalm tones and recitatives. The melody there is minimal and is, indeed, modeled on the text and its punctuations (*flexa, metrum, punctum*).[3] The accent syllable-neume appears under various forms and according to determined criteria, as illustrated in the following examples drawn from Gregorian and Ambrosian monody.

Gregorian

1. In the tone of RE for the *Readings* (in chant books written on LA), and in the tone of DO of the *Passion*, the accent is preceded and followed by melodically lower syllables.

Tone of RE

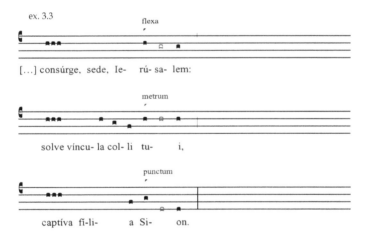

ex. 3.3

flexa

[...] consúrge, sede, Ie-   rú- sa- lem:

metrum

solve víncu- la col- li tu-   i,

punctum

captíva fí-li-   a Si-   on.

3. The *flexa* is the punctuation sign for the shortest phrasings. From the melodic point of view, it consists in a drop of the voice at the interval of a second, or of a minor third from the reciting tone, without a preparation tone and with an intermediate *epenthesis* (empty note). The *metrum* is the punctuation sign of the semi-phrase. Its melodic-rhythmic structure can be of one accent with or without a preparation note and with intermediate or anticipated *epenthesis*, or of a cursive type. The *punctum* is the punctuation sign for the end of a phrase and of a literary period, with a cadence of the same type as the *metrum*.

Tone of DO

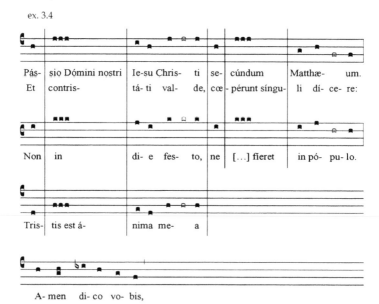

ex. 3.4

| Pás- | sio Dómini nostri | Ie-su Chris- | ti | se- | cúndum | Matthæ- | um. |
| Et | contris- | tá- ti val- | de, | cœ | - pérunt síngu- | li | dí- ce- re: |

| Non | in | di- e fes- | to, | ne | [...] fieret | in pó- pu- lo. |

| Tris- | tis est á- | nima me- | a |

A- men   di- co   vo- bis,

2. In the ferial tone of the *Pater noster*, certain accents of the text sing above the reciting tone (*dimittimus debitoribus, inducas*). So too at the cadence of the *punctum*, the accent syllable rises above the reciting tone, whereas the post-tonic syllable remains on it. At the cadence of the *metrum*, on the other hand, the accent syllable remains on the reciting tone, and the post-tonic syllable descends.

ex. 3.5   flexa

Præ-cép-tis sa-lu- tá- ri-bus mó- ni- ti:

                                    metrum   punctum

et di-	vína institutió-	ne for- má- ti,	au-	dé- mus dí- ce- re:
Pa-ter	noster, qui	es in cæ- lis:	sanctificétur	no- men tu- um;
	advéniat	regnum tu- um;		
	fíat vo-	lún-tas tu- a,	sic-	ut in cæ- lo
				et in ter- ra.
Pa-nem nostrum co-		ti- di- á- num	da	no- bis hó- di- e;
et di- mítte nobis dé-		bi- ta nos-tra,		

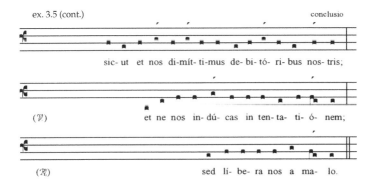

ex. 3.5 (cont.)

sic- ut et nos di-mít- ti-mus de- bi- tó- ri- bus nos- tris;

(𝒱) et ne nos in- dú- cas in ten- ta- ti- ó- nem;

(ℛ) sed lí- be- ra nos a ma- lo.

3. In the tones of the *syllabic genre*, corresponding to the punctuation signs of *flexa, mediatio*, and *terminatio*, the accent syllable is melodically more elevated than the final syllable.

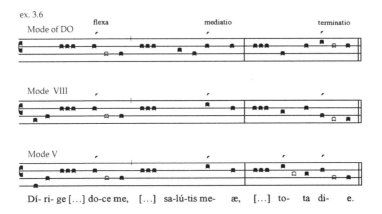

ex. 3.6

Mode of DO

Mode VIII

Mode V

Dí- ri- ge [...] do-ce me, [...] sa-lú-tis me- æ, [...] to- ta di- e.

4. In the *terminatio* of the semi-ornate tones of the Introits and Communions, modeled on the *cursus planus*,[4] the accent syllables are melodically more elevated than the final syllables.

4. The *cursus planus* is the simplest cursive cadence (= a harmonious succession of words at the end of a phrase, that produces a pleasurable effect due to the well-ordered layout of the tonic accents), formed by two paroxytone words, the second of which has three syllables. For example, *nóstris infúnde*; in *ætérnum cantábo*. In this type of cadence, the law of classical accentuation is respected: the tonic accent maintains the "principal role" in the melodic line.

ex. 3.7

5. In the Invitatory Tones with Psalm 94 the cadential accents of the *flexa* in Tone of Mode II are highlighted by the "*anticipation*" note on the preceding syllable.

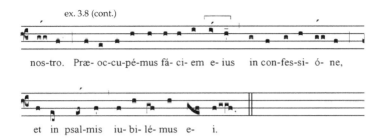

ex. 3.8 (cont.)

nos-tro. Præ- oc-cu-pé-mus fá- ci- em e- ius   in con-fes-si- ó- ne,

et in psal-mis   iu- bi- lé- mus e-   i.

6. In the Office antiphons the accent syllable is melodically more elevated than the others.

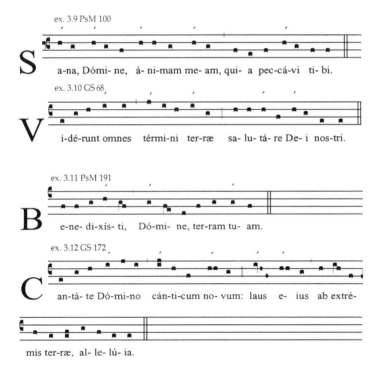

ex. 3.9 PsM 100

S a-na, Dómi- ne,   á- ni-mam me- am, qui- a pec-cá-vi   ti- bi.

ex. 3.10 GS 68

V i-dé-runt omnes   térmi-ni ter-ræ   sa- lu- tá- re De- i nos-tri.

ex. 3.11 PsM 191

B e-ne- di-xís- ti,   Dó-mi- ne, ter-ram tu- am.

ex. 3.12 GS 172

C an-tá- te Dó-mi-no   cán-ti-cum no- vum: laus   e- ius ab extré-

mis ter-ræ, al- le- lú- ia.

7. In the Introit antiphons of the Mass, melodic expansion is added to the melodically elevated accent syllables, this being the characteristic of the semi-ornate genre of these chants.

ex. 3.13 GR 91

(Rouse yourself! Why do you sleep, O Lord? Awake! Why do you hide your face? Why do you forget our affliction and oppression? For our soul is bowed down to the dust; our body clings to the ground. Rise up, come to our help!) Ps 44(43):23-26

Ambrosian

In the Ambrosian repertory, accent syllables in cadential contexts, as well as certain prominent accents within the text chanted on the reciting tone, are melodically more elevated than the final syllables.

1. From the *Laus magna angelorum*

ex. 3.14 GS 27

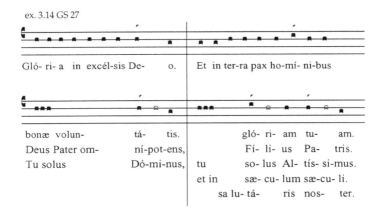

Gló- ri- a in excél-sis De-	o.	Et in ter-ra pax ho-mí- ni-bus	

bonæ volun-	tá- tis.		gló- ri- am tu-	am.
Deus Pater om-	ní-pot-ens,		Fí- li- us Pa-	tris.
Tu solus	Dó-mi-nus,	tu	so- lus Al- tís- si-mus.	
		et in	sæ- cu- lum sæ-cu- li.	
			sa lu- tá-	ris nos- ter.

2. From the *Credo*

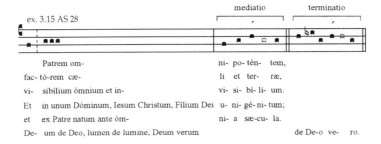

ex. 3.15 AS 28   mediatio   terminatio

	Patrem om-	ni- po- tén- tem,	
fac-	tó-rem cæ-	li et ter- ræ,	
vi-	sibílium ómnium et in-	vi- si- bí- li- um.	
Et	in unum Dóminum, Iesum Christum, Fílium Dei	u- ni- gé-ni- tum;	
et	ex Patre natum ante óm-	ni- a sæ-cu- la.	
De-	um de Deo, lumen de lumine, Deum verum		de De-o ve- ro.

3. From the *Præconium paschale (Exsultet)*

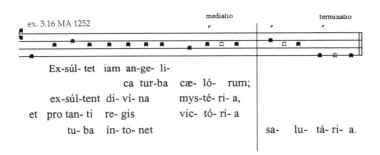

ex. 3.16 MA 1252   mediatio   terminatio

	Ex-súl- tet iam an-ge- li-			
		ca tur-ba	cæ- ló- rum;	
	ex-súl-tent di- ví- na		mys-té- ri- a,	
et	pro tan- ti re- gis		vic- tó- ri- a	
	tu- ba ín- to- net			sa- lu- tá- ri- a.

4. From the Prayers of Intercession (*Preces*)

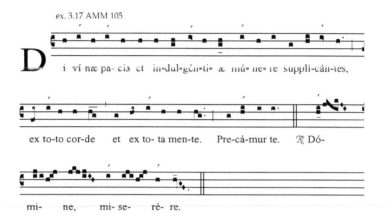

ex. 3.17 AMM 105

D i ví næ pa- cis et in-dul-gén-ti- æ mú- ne- re suppli-cán-tes,

ex to-to cor-de   et ex to- ta men-te.   Pre-cá-mur te.   ℟ Dó-

mi-   ne,   mi- se-   ré- re.

5. From the Office Antiphons

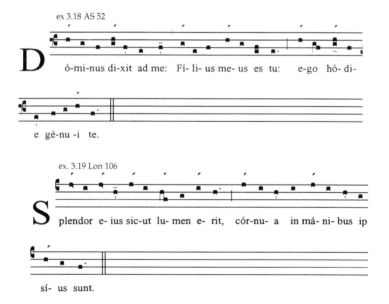

ex 3.18 AS 52

D ó-mi-nus di-xit ad me: Fí- li- us me- us es tu: e-go hó- di-

e gé-nu -i te.

ex. 3.19 Lon 106

S plendor e- ius sic-ut lu- men e- rit, cór-nu- a in má- ni- bus ip

sí- us sunt.

From the examples above, drawn from GREG and MIL, one
must not conclude that every accent syllable rigorously follows

a law of being more elevated than the other syllables. At times, because of the conceptual unity of the text, the melodic construction responds to a context greater than a single word, that of an entire phrase. This will be treated in the following chapter on the "*sostenuto*" style.

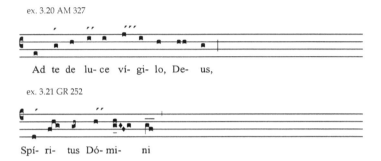

At times, it is the literary text that adapts itself to the melodic line of "fixed formulas," especially with the melody-types and the modal templates. For instance,

In the *centonized modal template* of Mode I, the accent is respected at the end of every incise, whereas the other accents can receive any syllable. In the fourth incise, in particular, it is placed in the redundant cadence.[5]

5. A *redundant cadence* is one in which the accent syllable of the last word rests on the same scale degree as that of the final syllable.

ex. 3.23 AM 640

In the *centonized template* of Mode I – II (ex.3.24–26), the accent is respected at the end of the redundant cadence of every incise, with the exception of the antiphon *Lex per Moysen*, because of the presence of the monosyllabic word.

ex. 3.24 AM 218

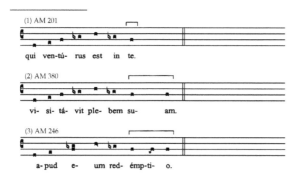

(1) AM 201

(2) AM 380

(3) AM 246

A second quality of the accent syllable is *brevity*. There is ample documentation of this by Latin authors of the classical[6] period, as well as from the period of Gregorian composition.[7] In fact, the brevity of the accented syllable is as frequent in Gregorian composition as that of its melodic elevation. For example:

6. Cf. Varro, *apud Sergium. De accentibus* (GL IV, fasc. II, p. 531, 23): "Acuta exilior et brevior et omni modo minor est quam gravis." (Translation: "The acute accent is light, more brief, and in every way less important than the grave accent.")

7. Cf. Pompeius (end of fifth century) in *Commentum. De accentibus* (GL V, p. 126, 27): "Acutus ergo dicitur, quando cursim syllabam proferimus. Circumflexus dicitur, quando <u>tractim</u> syllabam proferimus." ("The accent is named acute when the syllable is pronounced lightly. It is called circumflex when the syllable is pronounced with intensity.") In literary composition, the tonic accent on a long syllable carried the sign of the *circumflex accent* (the graphic combination of an acute accent and a grave accent). This means that the two accents, acute and grave, were each considered half of a long syllable (*Rô-ma = Róò-ma*).

1. Monosonic accent syllable followed by a bi-sonic final syllable

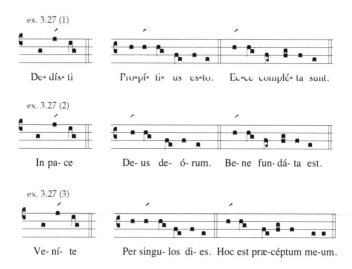

2. Monosonic accent syllable followed by plurisonic final syllable at the unison (*strophicus*)

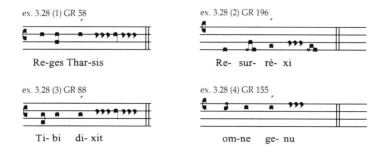

3. Monosonic accent syllable followed by an intermediate post-tonic syllable with a *strophicus*

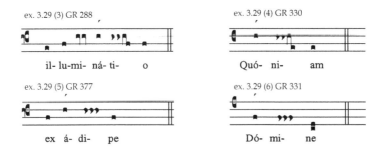

There are, in fact, entire compositions, like the one that follows, in which the monosonic accent syllable dominates.

(Remember your word to your servant, O Lord, / by which you have given me hope. / This is my comfort when I am brought low.) Roman Missal, cf. Ps 119(118):49-50

The brief, melodic character of the Latin accent syllable is not connected to the fact of the melodic ornamentation of these syllables, and this is true since the very origins of liturgical chant. The accented syllable does not necessarily ask for a greater ornamentation with respect to the others. For example, in primitive free hymnody, of which the Ambrosian *Laus magna angelorum* constitutes a rare and precious instance, the *iubilus* is placed on the final syllable of the penultimate phrase, and outside of the text.

ex. 3.31 AS 27

| Qui tol- lis pec-cá- ta mun-di, | mi- se- ré- re   no- bis. |
| Qui tol- lis pec-cá- ta mun-di, | sú- sci- pe [...]   nos-tram. |

The same phenomenon is found at the origins of psalmody: the soloist's melody (*iubilus*) of *in directum* psalmody is outside of the text. This can be observed in those fragments that have been passed down in the written tradition, namely, the versicles *Vespertina oratio* and *Dirigatur*.

ex. 3.32

℣ Vespertína orátio ascéndat ad te, Dó- mi- ne.

℣ Dirigátur, Dómine, orátio   me-   a.

Two observations should be made about this primitive psalmody. First, from these examples we cannot exclude the possibility of a performance practice that left the cantor free to add other notes within the cantillation of the text. Such a performance practice however, did not enter into the written tradition. Second, it seems that the *iubilus* might have no reference whatsoever to the text, or it may be a free invention of the soloist and refer merely to the reciting tone. In a successive phase, the ornamentation, with respect to the laws of accentuation of which we have spoken, seems to have been moved into the body of the text. This can be seen in the versicles *et in sæcula* and *Deus, in nomine.*

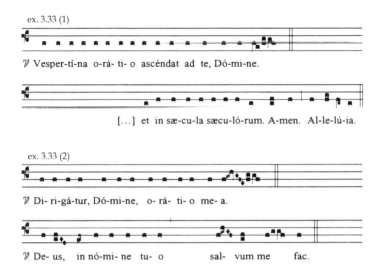

ex. 3.33 (1)

℣ Vesper-tí-na o-rá- ti- o ascéndat ad te, Dó-mi-ne.

[…] et in sæ-cu-la sæcu-ló-rum. A-men. Al-le-lú-ia.

ex. 3.33 (2)

℣ Di- ri-gá-tur, Dó-mi-ne, o- rá- ti- o me- a.

℣ De- us, in nó-mi- ne tu- o sal- vum me fac.

At this stage, given the dominant presence of the schola, the semi-ornate and ornate genres become the "rule" of compositional art. All the syllables of the text can then be the object of plurisonic melodic ornamentation, as can be observed in the Introit *Da pacem.*

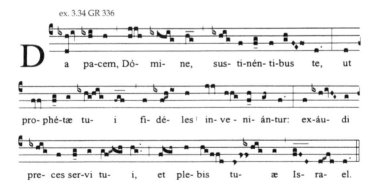

ex. 3.34 GR 336

D a pa-cem, Dó- mi- ne, sus- ti-nén- ti-bus te, ut

pro- phé-tæ tu- i fi- dé- les in-ve - ni- án-tur: ex-áu- di

pre- ces ser-vi tu- i, et ple- bis tu- æ Is- ra- el.

(Give peace, O Lord, to those who wait for you, / that your prophets be found true. / Hear the prayers of your servant, / and of your people Israel.)
Sir 36:18

One last observation on the quality of the accent syllable will conclude this section. The period of Gregorian composition is characterized by the phenomenon of the *Latin accentuation* of the postclassical period (fourth to fifth centuries). In this period, the accent syllable, understood as the *"anima vocis,"* maintains its melodic character with the addition of the qualities of intensity and brevity. In contrast to this, the qualities of *volume* and *weight* of the accent belong fundamentally to the Romantic period; that is, to the period of the Romance languages, the daughters of Latin. This period, which included the so-called *epoca romana*, witnessed the juxtaposition of the vocal technique of Gregorian chant with that of the polyphonic repertory. Dom A. Mocquereau, apropos of this, maintained that "the Roman accent has nothing in common with Gregorian Chant."[8]

3. The final syllable-neume

The unity and autonomy of a word are actuated and perfected on the final syllable, which represents the pole of relaxation. *Arsis* and *thesis*, which have their fulcrum on, respectively, the accent syllable and the final syllable, are complementary and signifying elements of the cohesion of a word's syllables. On the final syllable, the word comes to completion in its unity, meaning, rhythm, and, further still, in its melody and modality.

A. The melodic aspect of the final syllable

If a word's final syllable represents the pole of relaxation (*thesis*), it is normal that it be found in the lower part of the melodic arc. On its final syllable the word inclines in a more or less marked rhythmic pace, and then, cadences.[9] The Gregorian composer applies a variety of melodic treatments to the final syllable.

---

8. Cf. *Le nombre musical grégorien*, vol. 2, 232.
9. From the Latin *cádere* (to fall, sink, drop).

1. Monosonic, or simple, cadence

ex. 3.35

B e- ne-díc-tus Dó-mi- nus De us me us.

A *monosonic,* or *simple,* cadence is one in which the melodic-verbal unit on the final syllable consists of a single note.

A compelling example of the frequency of the monosonic final syllable can be found in the following Communion antiphon.

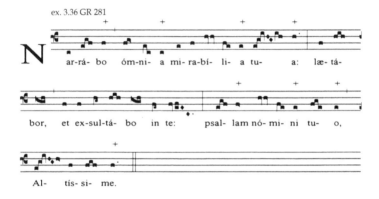

ex. 3.36 GR 281

N ar-rá- bo óm-ni- a mi- ra-bí- li- a tu- a: læ- tá-

bor, et ex-sul-tá- bo in te: psal- lam nó- mi- ni tu- o,

Al- tís- si- me.

(I will sing to the Lord who has been bountiful with me, / sing psalms to the name of the Lord Most High.) Roman Missal, cf. Ps 13(12):6

2. Plurisonic, or compound cadence

The *plurisonic cadence* is one in which the melodic-verbal unit is completed on the final syllable with the use of at least two notes. This cadence appears in the form of a *resolution* (cf. "*Hodie scietis*"), *ornamentation* (cf. "*Deus meus es tu*"), or *cadential expansion* (cf. "*Revelabi-tur . . . Domi-ni*" and "*in téne-bris*"). In the context of more than one melodic-verbal units, it functions as *oscillation* (cf. "*mendicare erubesco*") or as a *melodic connection* (cf. "*lætemur coram te*").

ex. 3.37

GR 38

Hó-   di- e sci- é-   tis,

PьM 60

De- us me- us es tu,

AM 594

et re-cor-dá- tus fú- e- ris

GR 40

Re- ve- lá- bi- tur   gló- ri- a Dó- mi- ni:

ex. 3.37 (cont.)

AM 210

se-dén-tem in té- ne- bris

AM 598

men-di-cá- re   e- ru- bés- co:

AM 195

læ- té-mur co- ram te   cor-de per-féc- to.

3. Redundant cadence

The *redundant cadence* is one in which the accent syllable of the last word of the musical phrase rests on the same scale degree as that of the final syllable. From a musical point of view, this final note is, in a certain sense, superfluous, or redundant, since the cadential note has already been sung on the accent syllable. The redundant cadence does not belong to the period of the primitive sources of liturgical chant, but rather to the period of the modal templates and of the centonized melodies. They were introduced into the compositions for the convenience of the composer, so as to avoid having to intervene on rigid formulas when adapting a text with one or more syllables in excess. Occasionally, the redundant cadence extends to more than one word.

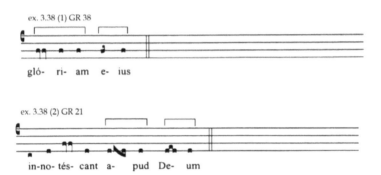

ex. 3.38 (1) GR 38

gló- ri- am e- ius

ex. 3.38 (2) GR 21

in-no- tés- cant a- pud De- um

Every melodic genre in Gregorian chant has its own form of re-dundant cadence. The syllabic genre has an *elementary* redundant cadence; the semi-ornate and ornate genres have, respectively, a *semi-ornate* and an *ornate* form. The following are some examples:

• *Elementary*: formed by only two notes, one for the accent and one for the final. With a *proparoxytone* word ("*véniet*"), the inter-mediate post-tonic syllable is ornamented by one or two notes, called the *intermediary epenthesis*.

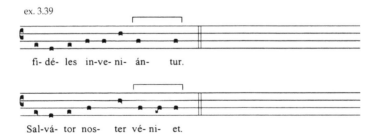

ex. 3.39

fi- dé- les in-ve- ni- án- tur.

Sal-vá- tor nos- ter vé- ni- et.

• *Semi-ornate*: when the accent and the final are ornamented by a small group of notes. In the case of a *proparoxytone*, the accent receives the note of the *anticipatory epenthesis* (in the examples indicated by an empty note).

ex. 3.40

• *Lowered*, or *falling*: when a melodic modification is made to the redundant cadence, with the last note(s) resting on a lower scale degree.

ex. 3.41

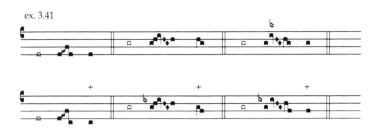

• *Ornate*: when the accent-neume and/or the final-neume contain(s) many notes (*melisma*).

ex. 3.42

(1) GR 128

me-   is.

(2) GR 148

cru-   cis.

4. Inverted cadence

In the *inverted cadence,* the melodic line of a typical cadential formula is inverted on the final syllable.

ex. 3.43

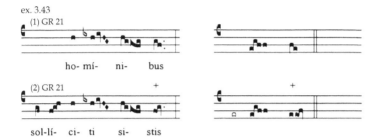

B. Modal aspect of the final syllable

The final syllable bears the structural solidity of a piece. The reason for this is, nearly always, that it carries the rhythmic weight as the pole of relaxation/*thesis* that closes the melodic-verbal unit. In literary construction, a word does not generally have absolute autonomy, but rather combines with others for grammatical reasons or conceptual unity (for instance, a noun with its adjective). Gregorian composers were familiar with Latin, understanding both the sense of the words and their rhythmic and phraseological unity, the substratum of literary construction. Therefore, within the context of a larger musical phrasing, some final syllables, while still maintaining the role of *thesis,* are subordinated to a successive pole of animation, represented by the accent syllable, the result being that within a composition there is a kind of hierarchy of final syllables. These melodic degrees highlight the modal framework that informs the phrasing, starting from the simpler units of the words up to that of the entire sentence.

The antiphon *Cantate Domino* presents four incises, excluding the added *alleluia* formula. Each contains two closely connected melodic-verbal units whose final syllable (*) is more important than the final syllable of the first word (+) of each because the first are subordinated to the successive accent.

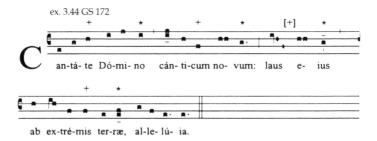

ex. 3.44 GS 172

Can-tá-te Dó-mi-no cán-ti-cum no-vum: laus e-ius

ab ex-tré-mis ter-ræ, al-le-lú-ia.

(Sing to the Lord a new song, his praise from the ends of the earth! Alleluia.) Isa 42:10

Clearly, the notes of the final syllables of the incises offer a modal framework of the antiphon, constructed, as they are within the scope of the modal fifth: RE - si, SI - sol. Echoing these modal degrees are those of the accent-syllables: RE - do / DO - la.

The final syllables are found on relatively lower scale degrees than those of the previous syllables, forming a pole of relaxation of a melodic nature. When seen in a broader context, though, that of an incise or phrase member, or an entire phrase, they can function like an "upbeat" or as a kind of "suspension," which is not only of a melodic nature, but also of a modal one. In other words, the final syllables will fall on notes that reveal the instinct and the art of the composer. In fact, in their melodic succession the composer assigns to these notes a modal role, more structural than melodic, and, consequently, one more intimately associated with the rhythmic order.

In *Antequam convenirent*, the final syllable of the first incise rests on the dominant LA. From there it descends to SOL, the cadence of the second incise, and then rests on FA, the cadence of the third incise. Finally, it closes on RE, the final redundant cadence, preceded by the subtonic DO before the *alleluia*.

(*. . . before they came together she was found to be with child by the Holy Spirit.*) Matt 1:18

Taken together, the above melodic and modal degrees of the final syllables form a pentatonic scale:

LA   SOL   FA   [   ]   RE   [DO]

major trichord
of the pentatonic scale

In the antiphon *Lapides torrentes*, the final syllables rest on the degrees of the modal fifth of *tetrardus*, beginning from the dominant and descending to the tonic SOL: RE - DO - SI - LA - SOL.

(*The stones of the torrent were sweet to him; all the souls of the just followed him.*) Source of text unknown

In the examples reported, the final syllables maintain the role of thesis in the melodic-verbal unit. They also carry the structural stability of the composition: upon them the melody rests, is stabilized and modalized. In brief, it is on the final syllable that the unity of the word, and groups of words, is realized, both from the melodic, and the modal points of view. From the final syllables of words is derived the modal framework of the composition.

4. Rhythmic interpretation

The text and the melody are *complementary elements* that coexist in perfect *symbiosis*, and are the primary sources of the melodic-verbal rhythm. Through them, Gregorian monody becomes the chant of the Word, a solemn and majestic declamation of a text, from which the melodies themselves obtain their expression of refined beauty.

Melodic-verbal rhythm consists, essentially, in the relationship between the poles of animation (*arsis*) and relaxation (*thesis*), represented, respectively, by the accent-neume and the final-neume.

Therefore, these are the fundamental factors that give form and life to the Word of the Gregorian melody: the aesthetic-modal combination of the sounds, and their coordination (*synthesis*) in the rhythm. From these factors is born a melodic-verbal style "*in legato*."

A. *The accent syllable-neume*

The characteristic of the Latin accent, as seen in the teachings of the ancient grammarians, is a fact of a melodic order (*tono*, "tone"). It is a factor of cohesion and of convergence that attracts and transmits the other syllables of the word toward the final syllable; its essence is to be a pole of animation (*arsis*) in movement toward the pole of relaxation (*thesis*) of the final. The rhythmic quality of the syllables that precede the final syllable derives from the accent syllable, whether that syllable is given a monosonic or a plurisonic sonorization.

The accent does not lose its quality as a pivotal point if it is placed between plurisonic neumes, and even less does it become an "upbeat" if it precedes a plurisonic neume. Consider the many instances of melodic-verbal accents of a single note in the following antiphon.

(The Lord Jesus, after eating supper with his disciples, / washed their feet and said to them: / Do you know what I, your Lord and Master, have done for you? / I have given you an example, that you should do likewise.)
Roman Missal, cf. John 13:12, 13, 15

In the antiphon *Exsultet spiritus meus*, the accent on s<u>pí</u>-ritus does not become an enclitic syllable of the following one with the *clivis*; it remains the point of convergence of melodic movement that reaches the strong tone of DO. From its position at the melodic apex, it gives momentum and color both to the syllables that precede it, as to the following ones on their way to the final.

The same is true for the accent on *Al-tís-simus* of the antiphon *Tu solus*, even though the note SOL is not the melodic apex.

ex. 3.49 PsM 189

Tu so- lus Al- tís-si- mus

The same is true at the beginning of a melodic movement where the accent of a single note, though secondary, always expresses an important attack, even when a plurisonic neume follows it. This attack is still more important when the initial note coincides with the structural note of the compositional context, as in the prospectus below, where SOL is the modal tone of the first incise. For this reason, in the paleographic sources the *virga* is marked with an episema.

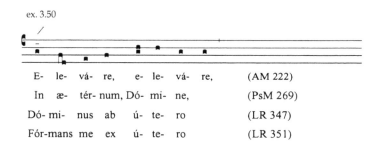

ex. 3.50

E-	le-	vá-	re,	e-	le-	vá-	re,	(AM 222)
In	æ-	tér-	num, Dó-	mi-	ne,			(PsM 269)
Dó-	mi-	nus	ab	ú-	te-	ro		(LR 347)
Fór-mans	me	ex	ú-	te-	ro			(LR 351)

The monosonic attack of a "fixed" formula, such as in the *incipit* of psalm tones, on the other hand, should be considered in the light of other criteria.

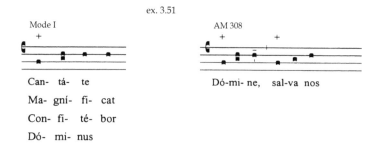

ex. 3.51

Mode I

Can- tá- te
Ma- gní- fi- cat
Con- fi- té- bor
Dó- mi- nus

AM 308

Dó-mi- ne,   sal-va nos

The formulas for the *incipit,* and the *terminatio,* of the psalm tones have a purely melodic significance. They are melodically mobile formulas that serve to connect the psalm tone to the attack and the ending of the antiphon to which they refer. Thus, the notes of the *incipit* are predisposed to accommodate all syllables of the psalter, regardless of their syllabic identity. That being said, a monosonic attack in whatever *incipit* of the psalm tones, carries the rhythmic connotation of syllabic value in a pre-tonic context. Other examples of a monosonic accent at the beginning of a piece are found in the melodies of the *Kyriale,* as follows:

ex. 3.52

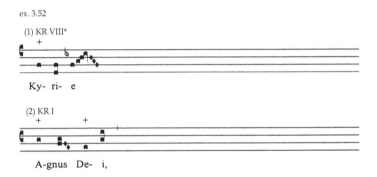

In these examples the monosonic attack of the two pieces coincides not only with the melodic-verbal accent of the word, but also with the structural melodic degree in the formulaic context. For this, it is not to be rhythmically subordinated to the plurisonic neume that follows it.

The textual accent sounded by a plurisonic neume responds to the normal conventions of Gregorian ornamentation. In the *syllabic genre,* the ornamentation of the accent is generally realized with neumes formed by a combination of the basic elements of notation, the grave accent and the acute accent. This can be seen in the modal templates with the procedure of *syneresis* that gives the word accent a *pes.*

ex. 3.53

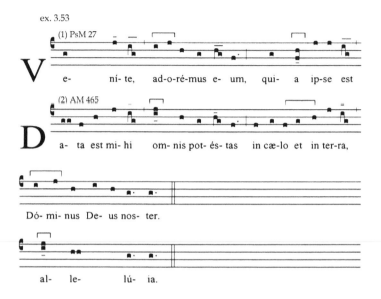

The neumes of two or three notes that form a homogeneous group (single group neumes) require a very legato vocal execution, that is, within a single impulse of the voice, with a syllabic articulation that begins gently, avoiding any intense vocal impulse within the neume. Their expressive quality must be subordinate to the larger context of the word, and, in the specific cases of a melody-type or of a modal template, subordinate to the phenomenon of *dieresis*.

In the *semi-ornate and ornate genres*, the more developed neumes (poly-group neumes) might contain elements that require a sonorous articulation qualitatively differentiated with respect to the others. The individuation and the interpretation of these differentiated elements is the object of study in the volume on *Neumatics*, in the chapter "Groupings Within the Neume."[10]

---

10. Cf. Alberto Turco, *The Musical Notation of Gregorian Chant*, Antiquæ Monodiæ Eruditio II,III (Verona: Edizioni Melosantiqua, 2006). The topics of the "development" of certain neumes, and of "articulation" within the neumes, are presented throughout AME vol. III.

B. The pre-tonic syllable-neume

The melodic movement of the pre-tonic syllables in tension toward the accent proceed in symbiosis with the verbal rhythm. Their attack must be soft and in tension, with a free movement, but without rushing. To avoid the danger of arriving on the accent rigidly and with intensity, nearly colliding with it, the preceding syllable must be sung with a graceful "holding back" (*trattenendo*) nuance. In the examples that follow, groups of two, three, and four pre-tonic syllables prepare for the neume of the melodic-verbal accent.

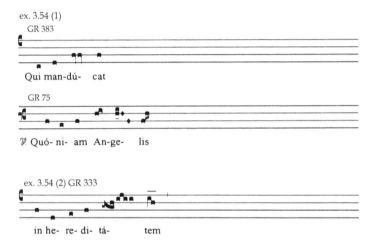

ex. 3.54 (1)
GR 383

Qui man-dú- cat

GR 75

℣ Quó- ni- am An-ge- lis

ex. 3.54 (2) GR 333

in he- re- di- tá- tem

Semiological facts often confirm the rhythmic criteria of these melodic contexts. In the intonation formula *ecce Rex veniet*, the oxytone *Rex* receives, precisely, the accent note of the formula. However, in order that this is not neglected, the St. Gall notation adds an *episema* on the top of the *virga*.

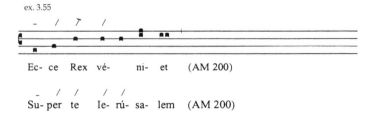

ex. 3.55

Ec- ce Rex vé- ni- et (AM 200)

Su- per te Ie- rú- sa- lem (AM 200)

C. *The intermediate post-tonic syllable-neume*

The intermediate post-tonic syllable presents itself primarily in *proparoxytone* words, usually in syllables with the vowels *e* and *i*. In syllabic genre, the intermediate syllable's rhythmic interpretation must accommodate the arrival on the final syllable with a calm and prepared articulation, avoiding a quick, or rushed, performance. Moreover, its attack must flow from the accent syllable, not only in relation to its vocal color but also to the quality of the articulation, which should arise without an impulse and in a legato manner. The antiphon *Omnipotens* offers a practical exercise on the correct interpretation of proparoxytone words.

ex. 3.56 AM 228

(Your all-powerful word leaped from heaven, from the royal throne. Alleluia.) Wis 18:15

The abovementioned interpretive criteria regarding the intermediate post-tonic syllable should be kept in mind when the first note of the intermediate post-tonic syllable involves a differentiated initial articulation with respect to the other notes (cf. *óf-fe*-rent).

ex. 3.57 GR 255

Whenever, then, the last note of a plurisonic neume on an intermediate syllable creates a melodic anticipation with the first note of the final syllable, the execution must be realized gently, distinguishing the syllables and avoiding a fusion of the unisonic sounds involved. Cf. the antiphon *Facta est.*

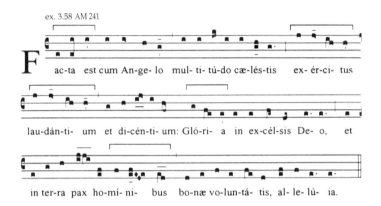

(And suddenly there was with the angel a multitude of the heavenly host, praising God and saying, "Glory to God in the highest, and on earth peace among those with whom he is pleased") Luke 2:13-14

D. *The final syllable-neume*

The rhythmic performance of the final note of a word does not require, per se, a "material duration" of the sound, but rather that the syllable be articulated "sweetly," letting it rest, giving the impression that something terminates and comes to a close in such a way that the words can be clearly distinguished without being disjointed. This kind of attention should always be given to a word's monosonic ending when followed by a plurisonic neume.

In a redundant cadence, from the rhythmic point of view, the pole of relaxation begins on the accent itself, which is then rhythmically prolonged toward the final syllable. The rhythmic interpretation of the accent must not be intensive, but, although it expresses the degree of the final of the melody, it must preserve the quality of the *anima vocis* of the pole of animation. It is to be sung and held in tension toward the final syllable.

E. Monosyllables

The monosyllables that do not have their own accents are joined to other words or grouped together to form pseudo-words of two or three syllables:

in térris   et in Sí- on   fác-tus est

et Dóminus   et vo-cá- bi- tur   do- cé- bit vos

                                      gé-nu- i te

In oratorical rhythm, monosyllables function like pre-tonic syllables, intermediary post-tonic syllables, and final syllables. However, monosyllables with their own accent and meaning become a rhythmical point of reference and may even create an intense syllabic articulation. With these monosyllables, the eventual final syllable maintains its function and quality within its melodic context.

ex. 3.59

"*Rex*": synthesis of the accent and the final

AM 200
a
Ec-ce Rex vé- ni- et

"*est*": final of a pseudo-proparoxytone
"*Rex*": accent of a pseudo-proparoxytone

AM 236
b
Ma-gni- fi- cá- tus est Rex pa- cí- fi- cus

"*pax*": final of a pseudo-proparoxytone

AM 243
c
et in ter- ra pax ho-mí- ni- bus

"*Rex*": pseudo-proparoxytone
"*est*": final of a pseudo-proparoxytone

AM 236
d
Rex pa- cí- fi- cus ma-gni- fi- cá- tus est,

5. The word-melody

As previously stated, the art of Gregorian composition elaborated three genres of melodic ornamentation of the literary word:
- *Syllabic*: syllables with primarily monosonic neumes
- *Semi-ornate*: syllables with plurisonic neumes, primarily single-group neumes
- *Ornate*: syllables with melismatic flowering of notes

In this last genre, the flowering of notes on a syllable (*iubilus* or *melisma*) takes the form of a literary word, articulated in *arsis* and *thesis*. Concrete examples of *word-melodies* are found especially in the melismas of the *Alleluia* of the Mass. The following are some examples.

The melody of this *Alleluia* (GR 375) consists of one *text-melody* (on the word *Alleluia*) plus four *word-melodies*. Of these four, the first contains six notes, plus the initial note of the *iubilus* on the final syllable of *alleluia* (SOL); the second contains six notes, plus the doubling of the note on the final syllable (SOL) and the *clivis*; the third contains six notes; the fourth contains six notes plus the cadential note of anticipation of the finale and its ornamental extension.

The melody of the *alleluia* of the modal template of Mode II (GR 49) contains one *text-melody* (on the word *Alleluia*) and five *word-melodies*. With the exception of the first word-melody, formed by five notes on the final syllable of *allelu-ia* up to the quarter bar, the others all contain four notes. After the last of these, characterized by the unison of the second note with the first, an ornamental cadential extension is added.

ex. 3.62 GR 16

A   l - le-   lú-   ia.

The *iubilus* (beginning with the last syllable of the *alleluia*) of the modal template of Mode VIII (GR 16) contains four word-melodies. The first, up to the quarter bar, has five notes. Beginning from the quarter bar, the next three word-melodies are formed by six notes, three notes, and six notes, not counting the doublings. Of particular interest is the melodic fragment of the first three notes of the last word-melody. This fragment is a transposed repetition of the penultimate word-melody. The abovementioned progression is, in turn, preceded by that of the first two word-melodies, of five and six notes, as if to constitute the continuation:

Do - Re - Do - La - Sol   Si - Do - [Sol] - La - Sol - Fa   La - Do - Si   Sol - Si - La - Sol

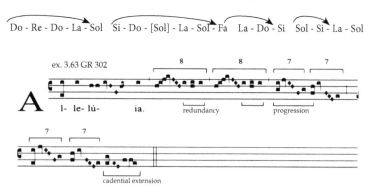

ex. 3.63 GR 302

A   l- le- lú-   ia.   redundancy   progression

cadential extension

The *iubilus* of this fourth *alleluia* (GR 302) is divisible in six word-melodies, plus the ornamental cadential extension. The first two of these have cadential extensions typical of a redundant cadence.

The following example, not from an *alleluia*, comes from the *iubilus* on the accent syllable of *A-ve* (GR 36). This *iubilus* contains four word-melodies of five and six notes, in alternation (a + a¹ + b + b¹).

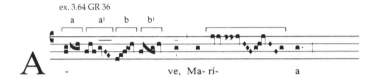

ex. 3.64 GR 36

The *iubilus* of the last verse of the Cant. *Cantemus Domino* (GR 187) consists of five word-melodies. The first two, of five notes each, are built on SOL, with the accent on DO; at the beginning of the second word-melody SOL is doubled.

The other three word-melodies, of five notes each plus a cadential extension, are built on the dominant DO. The link between these three word-melodies is made with a *clivis* (SOL - FA) and a *torculus* (SOL - LA - SOL).

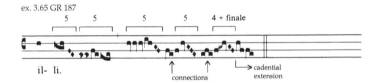

ex. 3.65 GR 187

As shown in the graph below, for clarification, in a melodic-verbal word, the pole of animation can be represented by a number of syllabic elements, whereas the pole of relaxation on the final consists of only one.

pole of animation						pole of relaxation
secondary accent				principle accent		final
				tér-		ra
				pó-	pu-	lus
			fi-	dé-		lis
			iu-	stí-	ti-	a
		a-	do	rá-		te
		de-	si-	dé-	ri-	um
	mi-	se-	ri-	cór-	di-	a
tri-	bu-	la-	ti-	ó-		nem

In a word-melody, on the other hand, the component parts of both the accent and the final can be expressed by a number of sonorous elements and are therefore not so easily recognizable. To define the poles of the word-melody, that is, of the accent and the final, it is necessary to refer to the modal-structural notes highlighted by the neumatic articulations (neumatic "breaks").

6. The reading of rhythm

Rhythmic interpretation in melodic-verbal style moves along a binary path: the correct articulation of the accent syllable-neume and the final syllable-neume, with the corresponding relationships of *arsis* and *thesis* represented by them.

Melodic-verbal rhythm tends fundamentally to the unity of each word. It is a question of movement—"ars bene movendi," says St. Augustine—based on the relationship of momentum and rest. Both the coloration typical of the accent syllable and the relaxed resolution of the final are born from that relationship. The accent syllable's important role has been sufficiently underlined by the position that it occupies in the context of the melody, and it does not need further emphasis here. Gregorian rhythm should be a smooth, supple placing of the syllables of a word, in the unity of their succession, a melodic-verbal synthesis that presupposes the assimilation of the Word concerning its literary diction and its spiritual meaning.

Naturally, melodic-verbal rhythm will use the physical and other particular qualities of certain sounds, as they emerge with intensity, volume or melodic development, always aiming to realize the functions of synthesis and of relation. Nevertheless, it does not identify with these. The sound represents only the material element of a melody. Melodic-verbal rhythm is a fact of *relationship*, primarily based on the principle of *Latin accentuation*. Dom J. Gajard, monk and choirmaster of Solesmes, writes:

> The true and essential nature of Latin accentuation does not lie in stress, which was added later as a corollary, but it is to be found in the relationship of impetus to fall between the accented and the final syllable. Whether in reading or singing, every time you have made this relationship between the accent and the final syllable of the word felt, your accentuation has been perfectly sound, even if you have hardly stressed the accented syllable. If, on the contrary, you have not made this relationship of rise and fall felt, your accentuation has been faulty or non-existent, however much you may have stressed the accented syllable. In fact, the more you stress and materialize this accented syllable, the more you isolate it from the other syllables, and, in consequence, the more you destroy the supreme aim of accentuation, which is to preserve the unity of the word.[11]

Therefore, a melodic-verbal entity is not born from the juxtaposition of one or more syllable-neumes to a cadence—this is only the material element—but from the relationship of one or more syllable-neumes *in movement* and *in tension* toward the cadence.

In the rhythmics of Gregorian chant, however, there is still another aspect to consider. Indeed, Gregorian rhythm is a fact of relationship between sounds, but it is a fact that must be perceived

---

11. Dom Joseph Gajard, *The Solesmes Method: Its Fundamental Principles and Practical Rules of Interpretation* (Collegeville, MN: Liturgical Press, 1960), 48.

by the *spirit*. It is a phenomenon of a *spiritual* nature, the indispensable condition for realizing both its rhythmical essence, and its primary quality of prayer and statement.

The keys to the reading of rhythm, therefore, are found in the text and in its *sound icon*, depicted by the paleographic musical notation, precisely, the adiastematic neumes above the text. This is the only way that the connection to the ancient oral tradition of Gregorian chant can be reestablished. In the last century, two formulations of Gregorian rhythm were developed: "*free measure*" rhythm, in the first fifty years, and following this, "*literary word*" rhythm. In the first formulation, the rhythm of the Gregorian melody is elaborated "abstractly," that is, without any reference to the literary text; the second formulation, on the other hand, begins from the fundamental principle that the Gregorian melody is built on the primary element of its literary text, and that its rhythm lives naturally on the verbal rhythm, from which it assumes its dynamic and its agogics.[12]

The birth of "*free measure*" rhythmics came about at the end of the nineteenth century with the publication of *Rythme, exécution et accompagnement du chant grégorien* (1892) by Fr. André-Antonin Lhoumeau. The systematic elaboration of this system, however, came in the first volume of Dom A. Mocquereau's *Le nombre musical grégorien ou rhymique grégorienne*, published in 1908. In the first part of this volume, it is affirmed that rhythm is determined by a succession of measures of two or three pulses. From here comes its incorrect denomination as "free rhythm," rather than as "free measure."

To facilitate the practical application of this system to the Gregorian melodies, Dom Mocquereau devised signs to be inserted into the VAT, the famous "rhythmic signs" of the editions

---

12. From the verb αγω (to lead, conduct, behave), from which comes the noun αγωγη (conduct, behavior). In general, *rhythmic agogics* means the conduct of rhythmical movement. In our specific case, when one affirms that the melodic rhythm must assume the agogics of verbal rhythm, it signifies that the melodic movement must model itself after the characteristics of verbal rhythm.

of Solesmes: the quarter bar, the comma, the vertical episema, the horizontal episema and the dot. The horizontal *episema*, placed on the *clivis*, is derived from the manuscript sources; the others, placed at the end of verbal and melodic elements and that function as punctuation of the Latin text and of the melodies, can be considered an amplification of preexisting signs (bar lines). Two of these, the vertical *episema* and the dot, assume, however, a significance that is purely theoretical, insofar as they were applied beyond the contexts mentioned above, indicating subdivisions of the melody in binary and ternary groups. Specifically, the vertical episema has the function of clarifying the binary and ternary subdivisions coinciding with the *arsic* and *thetic ictus*; the function of the *dot* is to double the time value of the note.

These two signs are not only of recent graphic invention, related to the bar lines of modern semiography, but more so, they deviate from the long tradition of Gregorian semiography. Dom Mocquereau's is an abstract didactic system of rhythm since it neglects the concrete musical facts so as to generalize them in theoretical and *a priori* schema that can then be applied to the melodies. In art, true interpretation can have, if one wants, recourse to didactic canons, but only as a point of departure; it must reach beyond to surpass simplistic and generalized rules, and ground itself on concrete facts, infinitely varied and always original.

Dom Mocquereau himself recognized twenty years later, in a certain sense, exactly how empirical the theory of free measure in the rhythmic interpretation of the Gregorian melodies was, with the publication of the second volume of *Le nombre musical grégorien*, in which the system of free measures is placed in relation to the "literary text." In the following example, the case is given of a final syllable of a word with a single note rhythmically connected and subordinated to the last note of a preceding plurisonic neume,[13] so that the note of "anticipation" of the final becomes the note that carries the rhythmic *ictus*. But this is nothing less

13. Cf. A. Mocquereau, *Le nombre musical grégorien, ou, rythmique grégorienne, théorie et pratique*, vol. 2 (Rome and Tournai: Desclée, 1908), 460.

than the negation of the natural connotation of the syllables of a word, and the final syllable at that, as well as of the text-melody symbiosis.

ex. 3.66

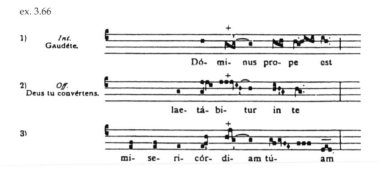

In the following table,[14] on the other hand, it is proposed that the final syllable of a proparoxytone can be rhythmically grouped either to the post-tonic intermediate syllable to form a binary measure, or to the last note of a plurisonic neume on an accent to form a ternary measure.

ex. 3.67 (1)

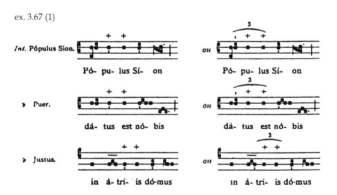

14. Ibid., 490.

ex. 3.67 (2)

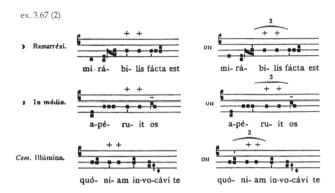

Faced with these two possibilities of grouping the sounds in binary or ternary measures, Dom Mocquereau concludes: "Practically, we must choose; a perfect performance demands it, and also the accompaniment."[15] In order to be credible, it must be said, the performance demands above all that the syllables of the text and the ornamentation notes of the melody maintain their natural connotation.

Another example, from the In. *Rorate cæli* (GT 34), will again underline the contradiction between a succession of free measures and a succession of melodic-verbal entities.

ex. 3.68 GR 34

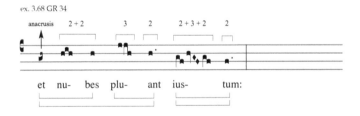

The phrase member *et nubes pluant iustum* is composed of three melodic-verbal units that should be rhythmically connected to one

---

15. "Pratiquement, il faut choisir; une exécution parfaite le réclame, et aussi l'accompagnment." Ibid., 490.

another in light of the criteria of conceptual unity. In this phrase member, the accent syllables are melodically semi-ornate, whereas the final syllables are monosonic. Just the same, the rhythmic chain of the three melodic-verbal units is realized by means of the monosonic neumes. The final syllable of "*nu-bes*," though moving toward the melodic accent of "*plu-ant*," maintains the connotation of a "final syllable of a verbal unit"; the final syllable of "*plu-ant*" is an important cadential articulation, since it is preceded by a note of anticipation and is found at the close of a conceptual unit between subject and verb. This cadential articulation is not, however, autonomous in the absolute sense, because from it flows the accent syllable of the word "*ius-tum*," with which the conceptual unity of the semi-phrase completes; to conclude, the final syllable of "*ius-tum*" terminates the composition of the phrase, with three finals of different rhythmic quality, and of growing importance, as they gradually proceed to the last.

To the three abovementioned melodic-verbal units correspond eight rhythmic measures of Dom Mocquereau: the first unit (*et nubes*) is subdivided in two binary measures, the first of which preceded by the anacrusic syllable *et*; the second unit (*pluant*) is subdivided in a ternary measure plus a binary; the third unit (*ius-tum*) contains two binary measures, and one ternary; at the end, the final syllable forms a binary measure. The connection, then, between the second and third melodic-verbal unit is rhythmically interrupted by the binary measure obtained by the *dot* on the final syllable of *plu-ant*. Moreover, the rhythm of the free measures is in sharp contrast to the meaning of the articulations of the plurisonic neumes on the accent syllables. In fact, the notes of each accent form a homogeneous whole, within which any rhythmic impulse (*ictus*) caused by the subdivision of the measures is absent. This is an interpretive aspect of the neume that is amply illustrated in the treatise on *Neumatics*.

Even if the rhythmic theory of free measures of Dom Mocquereau was credited with providing a positive response to the exigencies of interpreting Gregorian chant everywhere in the same way and by means of simple and easily comprehended notions, at the same time criticisms and objections were soon raised. In fact, in the Solesmes rhythmic editions of the post-Mocquereau period, the use of the rhythmic signs indicates a progressive abandonment of the system of free measures. This is evident in the three successive editions of the antiphon *In sanctitate*: AR of 1912 (ex. 1.15); AM of 1934 (ex. 1.16); and PsM of 1981 (ex. 1.17) on page 64. Above all, attention should be drawn to the different way of indicating the redundant cadences with the Solesmes rhythmic signs: in AR, the first note of the redundant cadence of the *incipit* (*In sanctitate*) is topped with a horizontal *episema*, and the second note with both a vertical and a horizontal *episema*; in AM, on the other hand, the first note has two *episemas*, whereas the other only one. This new way of highlighting the phrasing of a redundant cadence is within the logic of the etymology of this type of cadence, in which the accent syllable rests on the melodic degree of the final syllable.

That being said, one easily reads in AR and in AM that the use of the vertical *episema* is subordinated to the criteria of the succession of the free measures of two and three pulses (counts). In this view, it is assigned to the secondary accent syllable of *in sanc-titáte*; in the following incise, the AR prefers to underline the final syllable of the melodic-verbal unit of *serviá-mus*, whereas the AM prefers to underline the accent syllable of *Do-mino*, toward which the final syllable of *servia-mus* tends. Consequently, the position of the vertical *episema* preceding the abovementioned is also obligatory according to the logic of the succession of measures of two and three counts: in the AR, on the pre-tonic syllable of *ser-vi-amus*; in AM, on the accent syllable *servi-á-mus*. It also happens in the third incise (*et liberavit nos*), where AR and AM assign the vertical episema to the note of the accent syllable.

In PsM, the *episemas* and the *dot* are only used as signs of punctuation for the phrasing of the incises, of phrase members, and of phrases.

A. *The melodic-verbal and rhythmic units of the syllabic genre*

ex. 3.69 AM 291

M á- ri- a   et flú-mi-na,   be-ne- di- ci- te Dó-mi-no: hymnum

dí- ci- te, fon-tes, Dó-mi-no, al-le- lú- ia.

(Seas and rivers bless the Lord, fountains sing a hymn to the Lord.) Cf.
Dan 3:56

The antiphon *Maria et flumina* (Lauds of Epiphany), a textual
centonization drawn from the canticle of the three young men
(Dan 3), is subdivided in two phrase members, and can be traced
back to a responsorial form: *versus*, the first phrase member, *responsum*, the second phrase member. The first member is, in turn,
divisible in two incises, whose cadences can be defined as *mediatio*
and *terminatio*, like those in psalmody. Every incise is formed of
two melodic-verbal units. The Solesmes edition (AM) places a
quarter bar to indicate these.

$$\overset{\text{mediatio}}{} \qquad \overset{\text{terminatio}}{}$$

V. *Má - ri - a   et ⌈flú - mi - na,⌉ | be - ne - dí - ci - te ⌈Dó - mi - no:⌉*

The end of the first incise is characterized by an inverted cadence
of ornate genre, whereas the other three cadences are "simple"
(monosonic): *Mária, benedícite, Dómino*. The cadence on *Domino*
is a redundant cadence of resolution, while those on *Maria* and on
benedicite are cadences of preparation for the accent. The accent
syllables are melodically more elevated than those of the finals,
and put together they trace a melodic arch: FA – SOL, SOL - LA.

The second phrase member comprises five melodic-verbal
units, not divisible however in incises for reasons of the conceptual unity of the text. A quarter bar might have been justified only
after the cadential syllable of *Domi-no*, whose note is provided

with the Solesmes signs of the horizontal *episema* (above) and the vertical *episema* (below).

R. ⌐hym - num⌐ ⌐dí - ci - te,⌐ ⌐fon - tes,⌐ ⌐Dó - mi - no,⌐ ⌐al - le - lú - ia.⌐

The words *hymnum* and *fontes* are sung on two monosonic neumes at the unison, whose melodic contexts are comparable, from the aesthetic point of view, respectively, to a prosthesis and to an extension of a redundant cadence. Though in horizontal melodic contexts, the rhythmic unity of these words must still be realized by means of the synthesis of the animation of the accent syllable (*arsis*) and of the relaxation of the final syllable (*thesis*). The melodic arch traced by the relationship of the accent syllable and final syllable is the following:

si DO SOL SOL (mi) SOL fa (mi) RE fa SOL MI
hym - num   dí - ci - te,   fon -   tes, Dó - mi -no, al - le -   lú-ia

An observation regarding the melody of the *alleluia*: in a redundant cadence, when the accent occurs on the note of the redundancy, the preceding accent can receive any syllable.

ex. 3.70 ND 14

D if-fú-sa est grá- ti- a   in lá- bi- is tu-   is, propté- re- a ǀ be-ne-

dí- xit te De- us in æ- tér-num.

(Grace is poured upon your lips; Therefore God has blessed you forever.)
Ps 45(44):2

The text of the ant. *Diffusa est* (from the first Nocturn of Christmas) forms one musical phrase, divided in two members, as is well indicated by the half bar.

Each member consists of four melodic-verbal units. The two *episemas* assigned to the final syllable of *gra-ti-a* and to *benedixit te*, provide the possibility of another distinction within each member of two incises. The subdivision into incises is not indicated with the quarter bar for reasons of the conceptual unity of the text.

First phrase member:

Dif - fú - sa est   *grá - ti - a*   *in   lá - bi -is*   *tu - is,*

In this first member, the words *labiis* and *tuis* form a single rhythmic unit, in which the melodic accent comes on the redundant note. The first two units contain a melodic movement contrary to that of the text: the note of resolution of the final syllable is melodically higher than the others. In their rhythmic interpretation, the final syllable combines in a single pole the function of tension, attracting to itself the preceding syllables, and of resolution of the melodic-verbal unit.

The third melodic-verbal unit (*in labiis*) repeats, one step lower, the melody of the first unit (*diffusa est*); but, on the final syllable of this third unit, the principal melodic accent and the cadential resolution are shifted to the redundancy on the pronoun, satisfying the conceptual unity. It is important to underline in this first member that, put together, the melodic degrees of the finals of the melodic-verbal units form the major trichord plus the melodic degree under the *pien* of the pentatonic scale: LA-SOL-FA-RE.

Second phrase member:

prop - té - re - a   *be- ne- dí- xit te*   *Dé- us*   *in æ- tér- num.*

In this second phrase member the melodic line of the first member is restated, but in reverse. The first unit repeats the melodic design of *diffusa est*; beginning with tonic degree RE to then rest on FA. In the second unit, the pole of animation, with its accent on the melodic degree FA, has an anticipation of the melodic apex of the secondary accent of the first pre-tonic syllable *be-nedixit*. The melodic-verbal unit closes on the degree of the subtonic DO with the monosyl-

labic final *te*, creating a pseudo-proparoxytone. The third and fourth
melodic-verbal units (*Deus and in æternum*) proceed symmetrically
with the first two, but in a descending melodic progression, rising
stepwise with a melodic movement, contrary to that of the text, arriving on the secondary melodic accent of *in* on SOL, to then descend
and conclude with the redundant cadence on RE.

This phrase member involves an important articulation of resolution at the end of the second melodic-verbal unit (*benedixit te*).
The same type of resolution, though of minor importance, happens at the end of the first unit (*propterea*). The neume of the final
syllable of *De-us* is, instead, the *syneresis* of two monosonics, and
should be interpreted with an articulation of melodic connection.

B. The melodic-verbal units, and the rhythmic units, of the semi-ornate genre

The In. *Puer natus est nobis* (Mass of the Day of Christmas)
comprises three phrases, the first and third of which divide in two
members (cf. the half bars).

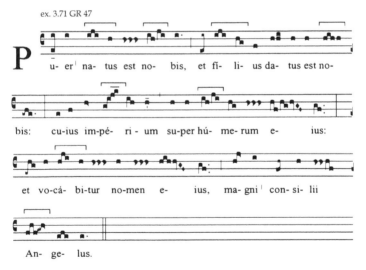

ex. 3.71 GR 47

*(A child is born for us, and a son is given to us; / his scepter of power rests
upon his shoulder, / and his name will be called Messenger of great counsel.)*
Roman Missal, cf. Isa 9:5

First phrase:

first member: ⌐Pu- er⌐ ⌐na- tus est⌐ [tus est] ⌐no- bis,⌐

second member: ⌐et ⌐ fi- i- ⌐ us⌐ ⌐da- tus est⌐ ⌐no- bis:⌐

Each member is formed of three melodic-verbal units, presenting a parallel melodic structure. To *puer natus est* is matched the melody of *et filius datus est*, and to the first *nobis*, with the accent of four notes and final cadence on the dominant (RE), is matched the second *nobis* with the accent on DO (the dominant of "repose"), and the final descending cadence on SOL (tonic). The ornamentation of four notes for the accent is common to all of the melodic-verbal units: *natus* and *nobis, datus* and *nobis,* and *filius* with a fifth note providing a melodic connection.

Second phrase:

⌐cu- ius im- pé - ri- um⌐ ⌐su- per hú- me- rum⌐ ⌐e- ius:⌐

In this phrase again three melodic-verbal units are present, bearing in mind that the relative pronoun *cuius* is situated within a pre-tonic context and the adverb *super* plays the part of a prosthesis. The accent syllable of *impé-rium* and of *hú-me-rum* are ornamented with four notes, just as those of the preceding phrase, which are then followed by two notes for the intermediary post-tonic syllables, the second of which has the role of anticipation of the final (*impé-ri-um*) and of oscillation (*hú-me-rum*). The ornamentation of *eius*, on the other hand, is richer: seven notes for the accent and two for the cadence.

Third phrase:

first member: ‖ et   vo- ca- bi- tur ‖ no- men ‖ e- ius,

second member: ‖ ma- gni ‖ con- sí- li- i ‖ Án- ge- lus.

The ornamentation on vocabitur, preceded by the re-intonation on *et* (*torculus initio debilis* of intonation), is comparable to that on *humerum*. The intermediary post-tonic syllable does not have a *clivis* with the second note on SI because this is anticipated by the intonation *torculus* on *et*. The melody on *nomen* is nothing but the extension of *vocabitur*, which creates a melodic connection with *eius*, whose accent melody is similar to that of *eius* after *humerum*. In the second member the accent on *má-gni* represents the last melodic apex of the piece; it is ornamented with two notes, like that of *pú-er*. The ornamentation on the accent of *consí-li-i* (on the intermediary post-tonic syllable as an anticipated *epenthesis*) and the accent of *Án-gelus* is both times of four notes. The piece concludes with a redundant cadence, in which the accent syllable of *Ángelus* plays the part of an anticipated *epenthesis*.

C. *The melodic-verbal and rhythmic units of the ornate genre*

The text of the Of. *Super flumina* is drawn from the first verse of Psalm 136. It forms a single phrase, divided in three members:

First member   *Su-per flu-mi-na Ba-by-lo-nis*

Second member   *illic sedimus, et flevimus,*

Third member   *dum re-cor-da-re-mur tu-i, Si-on*

Each phrase member of the literary text constitutes one melodic phrase, which, in turn, can be divided in two members because of the rich ornamentation.

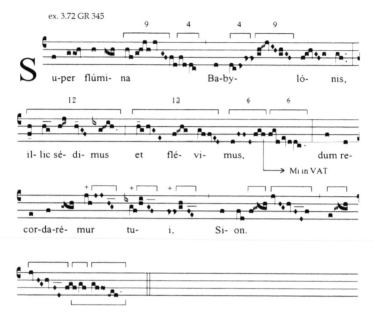

ex. 3.72 GR 345

(*By the waters of Babylon, there we sat down and wept, when we remembered Zion.*) Ps 137(136):1

First member:

Su- per flú- mi- na   Ba- by- ló- nis,

The two melodic-verbal clauses above are divided by a quarter-bar. The first is constructed in semi-ornate genre situated within the text; the *iubilus* on *flumina*, on the other hand, is on the final syllable, that is, not within the word. The word *Babylonis*, however, has an ornate melodic construction within the text, on the syllable that precedes the syllable of the redundant accent. Each *iubilus* is made of two word-melodies: the first with nine and four notes, the second with four and nine notes.

Second member:

| ‾il- lic   sé- di- mus,‾ | ‾et   flé- vi- mus,‾ |

Again, two melodic-verbal units, which, since the text permits it, are justly divided by the half-bar into two members. These two units have the same literary construction of the preceding member:

super flumina (preposition of two syllables plus a proparoxytone)

illic sedimus (adverb of two syllables plus a proparoxytone)

Babylónis (four syllables)

et flévimus (four syllables)

The ornamentation within the text lies somewhere between a semi-ornate and an ornate genre. The allocation of the notes within the syllables of the text is not casual: the first unit is formed of twelve notes; the second, also of twelve notes, excluding the *iubilus* of the final syllable, which is also formed of two word-melodies of six notes each,[16] for a total of twelve notes, not counting the doublings.

Third member:

| ‾dum   re- cor- da- ré- mur‾ | ‾tu- i,‾ ‾Si- on.‾ |

The third member has three melodic-verbal units. The ornamentation within the text is of the ornate genre, with the exception of the pre-tonic syllabic context of the first unit. The ornamentation of the syllables was done with the repetition of the same fragment of four notes, in a descending melodic progression in which,

---

16. It was not by chance then, that the last note of the first word-melody oscillated over time, descending to MI.

however, the higher strong tone DO has absorbed the semitonal note SI. This fragment oftentimes flows directly from the *clivis*, in a descending melodic progression and, in the lower range, with the semitonal MI of the *clivis* absorbed by FA. The piece concludes with the large *iubilus* on the final syllable of "*Si-on*." This is composed of four word-melodies, that repeat, two by two, the same melodic arrangement—with the exception of the MI, foreign to the context—to which follows an extension of cadential nature of another two word-melodies.

CHAPTER 4

MELODY (Part II)

1. *Sostenuto* melodic-verbal style

The analysis of the *single word* allows us to understand only the most simple forms of the art of Gregorian composition and the basic elements of the science of rhythm. Yet, the words of a literary text are selected and arranged to express concepts that go beyond their particular significance, and which can be fully grasped only in the broader context of their setting. It happens the same way in a musical construction. Sounds are arranged within a compositional context capable of expressing a complete musical idea. The rhythm creates a synthesis of textual and musical elements crafted to let the content emerge. It is the rhythm that grasps the various conceptual units by means of the synthesis of two, three, or more words, and even the content of a whole piece with the synthesis of incises and phrase members. The rhythmic syntheses achieved within a piece are commonly called *rhythmic punctuation*, or better still, *phrasing*.

Thanks to the text-melody symbiosis, it is rare to encounter discrepancies in Gregorian chant between textual punctuations and melodic punctuations: "Cantillation (melody) subdivides in the same way as the text."[1]

1. Cf. Hucbald of Saint-Amand, *De Harmonica Institutione*, in SE, p. 125. *Eodem modo distinguitur cantilena, quo et sententia.*

The analysis of the incise, the phrase member, or of the phrase, must still not lose sight of the analysis of the *word*. These greater contexts can be equated to *large words*, in which the pole of the melodic-verbal accent will correspond to the apex and the melodic antecedent (*protasis*), and the pole of the final will correspond to the consequent (*apodosis*). Like the word, so too the incise, phrase member and phrase create an arch-form melodic line. However, an additional fact must be considered in the rhythmic synthesis of a phrase: the finals of the words do not descend below the arch of the melodic line. Instead, they rest on the modal degrees that progressively lead to the apex and then to the final cadence. Due to this aspect of the art of Gregorian composition, the style of the entire phrase is more greatly supported and sustained (i.e., *sostenuto*) by the rhythmic synthesis.

In the following example, the *sostenuto* style can be observed between the noun and possessive adjective of *orationem meam*. It is achieved by the articulation of the neume of two notes at the unison (*bivirga*) on the final syllable of *oratio-nem* that tends to the melodic accentuation of *meam*. The notes on the dominant DO express a crescendo towards the melodic apex, represented by the phraseological accentuation of *meam*: DO appears first as a note of ornamentation (|), then as a melodic-verbal accent (+), then as a doubled DO (*bivirga*, ++) that functions as a rhythmic pole attracting to itself the preceding syllables and generating the accentuation on *meam*.

ex. 4.1 GR 115 | +   ++

Ex-áu-di, De- us, o- ra- ti- ó- nem me- am,

(Give ear to my prayer, O Lord.) Ps 55(54):1

In the following example, on the other hand, the *sostenuto* style comes about between the melodic-verbal units. The final syllables of these traces a melodic arch $\overset{\frown}{\text{FA}} - \text{SOL} - \text{LA} - \overset{\searrow}{\text{FA}}$, reinforcing the connection between them. The accentuation of *omnium* on the dominant LA is prepared by the accent of *mise-re-ris*. The ornate cadence on *Domi-ne* remains on FA, from which point begins the successive phrase member.

ex. 4.2 GR 62

Mi- se- ré- ris óm- ni- um, Dó- mi- ne, et ni- hil

(You are merciful to all, O Lord.) Roman Missal, Wis 11

Finally, we can observe the *sostenuto* melodic-verbal style in an entire piece, the In. *Gaudete in Domino*, in which the final syllables of words provide the structure of a melodic-modal arch form.

ex. 4.3 GR 21

G au-dé- te in Dó- mi- no sem- per: í- te- rum di- co,

gau- dé- te: mo-dés- ti- a ves- tra no-ta sit óm-ni-bus ho-mí-

ni- bus: Dó-mi- nus pro- peest. Ni- hil sol- lí- ci- ti

si- tis: sed in om- ni o- ra- ti- ó- ne pe- ti- ti- ó- nes ves-

træ in-no- tés- cant a- pud De- um.

(Rejoice in the Lord always; again I say, rejoice. / Indeed, the Lord is near.) Roman Missal, Phil 4:4-5

The textual theme of this *introit* is synthesized in the first phrase, in which the modal tones on the final syllables provide resolution to the melodic-verbal units, RE - FA - SOL - LA - FA - RE, and form an arch construction, and are then taken up again in the three following phrases.

First phrase: RE/FA - [SOL] - LA - FA - RE.

> *Gaudete* (RE) *in Domino semper* (LA) *iterum dico* (FA), *gaudete* (RE)

Second phrase: FA - LA - [SOL] - LA - FA.

> *modestia* (FA) *vestra* (LA) *nota sit omnibus* (LA) *hominibus* (FA)

Third phrase: LA - FA/SOL.

> *Dominus prope est* (LA) *Nihil* (LA) *solliciti sitis* (SOL)

Fourth phrase: DO - SOL - DO - RE

> *sed in omni* (DO) *oratione* (SOL) *petitiones vestræ* (DO) *innotescant* (RE) *apud* (RE)

This analysis, extending to the whole piece, illustrates the *great rhythm*, which is determined, first of all, by identifying the melodic-verbal units and grouping them into one or more phrase members in light of the symbiosis of the text and melodic construction. One proceeds then to the determination of the melodic apex within the phrasing of each member. Next, follows the individuation of the phrase-rhythm and its melodic apex. The final step, in the pieces with a number of phrases, is the determination of the over-arching apex, that surpasses melodically all the others. In the following example, the apex of the phrase member is marked with one accent, those of the phrase and of the entire piece are marked, respectively, with two accents and three accents.

ex. 4.4 GR 78

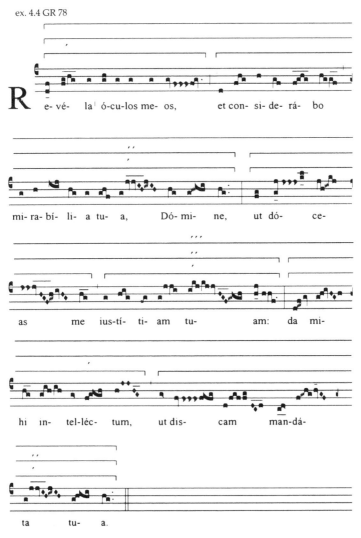

(Open my eyes, and I will consider your wonders, O Lord, that you may teach me your righteousness: give me understanding, that I may learn your commandments.) Cf. Ps 119(118):18, 26, 73 [A textual variant consisting of the ancient incipit "Revela" (cf. GT) is reproduced here in place of "Levabo" as reported in GR 78.]

One should not think that every piece in the Gregorian repertory will create a symmetrical melodic construction, taking into
account the apex of every phrasing within. There are a number of
pieces in which the melodic line is rather "horizontal." It is important, then, that the analysis and synthesis of the greater rhythm
will uncover the melodic progressions proper to each piece: cf.
the In. *Lætetur cor.*

ex. 4.5 GR 268

*([L]et the hearts of those who seek the LORD rejoice. / Seek the LORD and
his strength; / seek his presence continually.)* Ps 105:3-4, NRSV

2. Phrasing in the syllabic, semi-ornate, and ornate genres

A. *The syllabic genre*

In the Ant. *Sana, Domine,* the composition of three incises (a +
a + b) contains seven complete simple melodic-verbal units, that
is, with monosonic neumes.

ex. 4.6 PsM 100

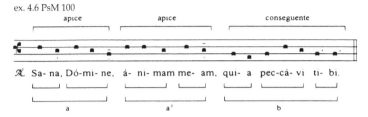

(Heal me [Lord] for I have sinned against you.) Ps 41(40):4

In this antiphon, the relation between the pole of tension and the pole of relaxation is given by the articulation[2] of the accent and of the cadence. Just the same, not all of these melodic-verbal units with their articulations carry the same importance within the phrase. Some of them should be considered subordinate to others, because of their melodic and textual unity. The words *quia peccavi tibi* create a single formulaic unity, in which the articulation of the accent comes on the redundant cadence of *tibi* and, previously, on the accent syllable of *peccávi*.

The articulation of the final of *qui-a* enters into the *pre-tonic* context leading to the accent syllable of *peccávi*. The final syllables of *sa-na* and of *ani-mam* preserve their autonomy, but are oriented toward the principal accent of *Dó-mine* and of *mé-am*, realizing in this way the conceptual unity of the incise. The complete meaning of the text's principal phrase comes with the union of the incises a and a' (doubling of the same melody). There is no quarter bar after the word *Domine* for this reason, but the final syllable-neume receives two *episemas*, the sign, that is, for the phrasing of the incise. The articulations of final syllables, on which the rhythmic and verbal unity are realized, should also be interpreted in relation to the role they play in the phrase.

---

2. The term *syllabic articulation* signifies the passage from one syllable to another. So too in the word-melodies the relational phenomenon between sounds might correctly be indicated with the term *neumatic articulation*.

The principal rhythmic articulations of the final syllables are realized with the word *meam* (end of the first phrase member) and *tibi* (end of the phrase); the others are interpreted in relation to the abovementioned. The final syllables of *me-am* and of *ti-bi* must complete rhythmically in such a way as to highlight, respectively, the resolution of *dissolvency*[3] of the phrasing of the semi-phrase and of the phrase; the final syllables of *sa-na* and of *ani-mam*, while having the function of completing the various rhythmic and verbal units, are subordinated to provide completion to a larger phrasing, through resolution of the melodic-verbal resonance by *absolvency*. The final syllables of *qui-a* and of *pecca-vi* are parts, respectively, of the rhythmic pre-tonic context, and the context of movement toward the cadential resolution.

The composition evolves with a horizontal melodic design: it begins directly, two times with the same melody (a and a'), at the apex, followed by the consequent phase.

The modal configuration confirms this rhythmic analysis. The antiphon is composed of two phrase members, of which the first is formed by two equal incises (a and a'). The first incise cadences on the tonic RE, whereas the second cadences on the melodically suspended MI. The third incise (= second phrase member) terminates on the tonic RE. The accents, on the other hand, rest on the modal degree of the psalmodic tenor FA. The articulations of the incises, of the phrase members, and of the entire phrase should reflect the light of the melodic-textual phrasing and the modal analysis.

3. Solvency, used in this volume as a term describing a phonetic phenomenon, refers to the quality of the passage from one syllable to the next. This passage, also called "syllabic articulation," varies according to the types and combinations of vowels and/or consonants present in a particular syllabic articulation. It varies also in virtue of where the syllabic articulation occurs in the melodic phrase. The quality of the solvency can be described as being either in "dissolvency"—when the articulation closes a rhythmic unit, and the melody successively begins another; or as being in "absolvency"—when the final syllable concludes a rhythmic unit while at the same time being the point of departure for another, thus avoiding a new attack on the following word.

The Ant. *Nos qui vivimus* consists of a single phrase formed by two incises.

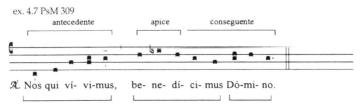

(But we that live bless the Lord.) Cf. Ps 115:17-18

In this antiphon, three melodic-verbal units can be individuated:

Nos qui vívimus | *benedicimus* | *Dómino.*

The first melodic-verbal unit consists of an intonation formula, beginning from below, that has as its center and pole of animation the accent-syllable of *ví-vimus*. The word's rhythmic unity completes with the final syllable. The monosyllables *nos* and *qui* are placed in the "formulaic" context of intonation, in the role of a pre-tonic syllable-neume.

Therefore, their rhythmic interpretation should be characterized by a fluid movement, without rushing, toward the accent, bearing in mind that the oxytone pronoun *nos* maintains its own accent and must not be considered an enclitic syllable (it would be better to assign the *vertical episema* to *nos* rather than to *qui*). The final syllable of *vivi-mus* is the second pole of the melodic-verbal unit, and the solution of the verbal articulation happens here. The rhythmic interpretation must give this syllable the character of a conclusive ending of the rhythmic movement with a clear and, at the same time, gentle articulation, that distinguishes it from the following syllable without shortening its syllabic value.

In the melodic-verbal unit of *benedícimus*, the accent-syllable (pole of animation) is preceded by two pre-tonic syllables, of which the first is on the same scale degree, the second an ornamentation of B-flat, and it is followed by an intermediary post-tonic syllable.

In this case, the interpretation must give the pre-tonic syllables a fluid, legato movement toward the accent, and to the intermediary post tonic syllable a gentle push toward the final, without colliding into it. The third melodic-verbal unit on *Domino* provides the pole of animation that includes the enlarged articulation of the accent (the two notes of the *pes*) and the intermediary post-tonic syllable.

In the second incise (*benedícimus Domino*), the accent-syllable of *Domino* is the phraseological accent and the fulcrum of the pole of animation. It follows that the articulation of the final syllable of *benedíci-mus*, oriented toward this accent, assumes the rhythmic connotation of a micro-articulation.

Having concluded this rhythmic analysis it is appropriate to draw attention to the phenomenon of the *solution, or rather the resolution,* of melodic resonance in the verbal articulation of *vivimus* in the first incise in relation to the context of the entire phrase.

The solvency of the melodic resonance of an articulation can result in two interpretations:

- in *dissolvency*, if the final syllable of *vivimus* closes a rhythmic unit and the melody begins again with another;

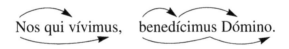

- or in *absolvency*, if the final syllable of *vivimus* is the point of linkage of a rhythmic unit that concludes, and at the same time is the starting point of a new one, avoiding an attack on the successive syllable.

The compositional context in question is more favorable to the second interpretation.

The Ant. *Habitabit* is formed by one phrase, subdivided in two members each comprising two incises. The composition is modally structured on MI, climbing to SOL for the melodic accentuation and for the psalmodic tenor.

ex. 4.8 PsM 16

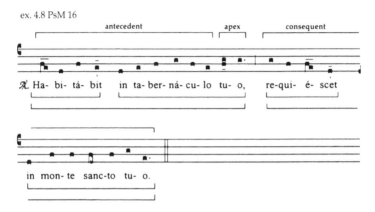

(He will dwell in your tabernacle, he will dwell on your holy mountain.) Cf. Ps 15(14):1

The antiphon has an arch-form melodic-modal structure, divisible in three phases: the *antecedent*, up to the accent of *taber-ná-culo*; the *apex*, on *tuo*; and the *consequent*, from *requiescet* until the end. The monosonic neume of the final syllable of the first and third incises (MI - RE), each with an *episema*, carries the role of the *pivot tone* for the connection of the successive incises, to be precise, the second and the fourth.

The rhythmic synthesis of the entire antiphon would require that the initial attack of the consequent phase on the apex (SOL) resume after a phraseological punctuation of "distinction," with the same dynamic connotation of the cadential resolution of *tuo*.

B. The semi-ornate genre

The In. *Inclina Domine* is composed of an arrangement of numerous formulas due to the length of its text; it contains three phrases, as indicated by the full bar lines.

ex. 4.9 GR 326

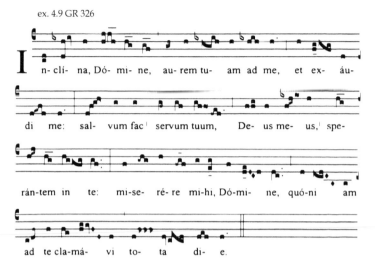

di me: sal- vum fac servum tuum, De- us me- us, spe-

(Turn your ear, O Lord, and answer me; / save the servant who trusts in you, my God. Have mercy on me, O Lord, for I cry to you all the day long.)
Roman Missal, Ps 86(85):1-3

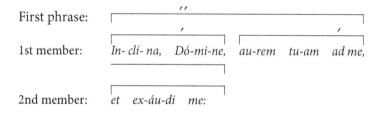

The first phrase contains two phrase members. The first is formed by four melodic-verbal units, since the possessive adjective *tuam* forms a single unit with the noun *aurem*, both from the textual point of view and from the melodic. The VAT subdivides this first member in three incises. The quarter-bar after the verb *inclina* seems excessive. The subdivision in two incises better reflects both the textual meaning as well as the melody. The second member is limited to a single melodic-verbal unit.

The cadences are simple (*inclina*), composite (*Domine*) and redundant (*tuam, ad me, exaudi me*). The phrase has a melodic arch-form construction, which, after the beginning and the conclusion in the lower register around RE, takes place almost entirely on the dominant LA. In the first member, the melodic apex of the first incise falls on the accent of *Dó-mine*, whereas that of the second incise, falls on the redundant cadential note on *ad me*. One can hardly speak of an apex in the second member, since the melody is already in motion toward the lower register and the accent of the redundant cadence. The phrase has its apex on the accent of *Dó-mine* and its phrasing foresees a single punctuation after the first member, on the redundancy of *ad me*, in which the articulation of the final note should be rhythmically performed in dissolvency. The simple cadences (*inclí-na* and *tu-am*) and the composite cadence of *Domi-ne* are both of the rhythmic resolution type, but in absolvency. The monosonic neume of the final syllable on *au-rem* carries the role of "pivot tone."

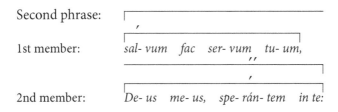

The second phrase consists of two phrase members, each divided in two melodic-verbal units. In the first member the apex falls on the accent of *sal-vum*; the monosonic neume of *fac*, final syllable of a pseudo-proparoxytone, carries the role of pivot tone connecting the two melodic-verbal units.

In the second phrase member, the melodic apex falls on the accent of *spe-rán-tem*. The monosonic neume of the final syllable of *me-us* acts as a connector of the two melodic-verbal units, in the rhythmic role of the resolution note in absolvency. The cadence of *in te* (LA - SOL, FA - SOL - FA) is comparable with the one on *tuum*, (SOL - FA, RE - MI - RE).

The arch-form melodic construction of the entire phrase ends on the dominant FA. The completion of the melodic arch happens in the third phrase.

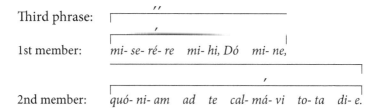

This last phrase, too, contains two phrase members: the first has two melodic-verbal units (*miserere mihi*, and *Domine*), and the second has three melodic-verbal units (*quoniam*, *ad te clamavi*, and *tota die*). The third incise is no more than an extension of the cadence of the second incise (*clamavi*), of the ornate redundant type.

The melodic apexes of the first member and of the second member are, respectively, the melodic-verbal accents of *mise-ré-re* and of *cla-má-vi*. On the accent of the latter falls the apex of the entire phrase.

It is not easy to establish the phraseological apex in this long piece. It seems, however, to possibly identify it in the second part of the text, at the melodic-verbal accentuation of "*mi-hi*." The note on the pronoun *te* has the role of "pivot tone," from which flows the pre-tonic syllable of *cla-mavi*.

C. *The ornate genre*

Ecce quam bonum is a *responsorium graduale*, the musical form of the responsorial psalmody of the Mass.

ex. 4.10 (cont.)

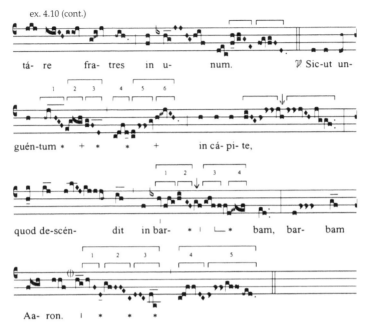

tá- re   fra- tres   in u-   num.   ℣ Sic-ut un-

guén-tum *   +   *   *   +   in cá- pi- te,

quod de-scén-   dit   in bar-   * | ∟ *   bam,   bar-   bam

Aa- ron. | *   *   *

(Behold, how good and pleasant it is when brothers dwell in unity! It is like the precious oil upon the head, running down upon the beard, upon the beard of Aaron.) Ps 133(132):1-2

The text is drawn from Psalm 132, verses 1 and 2, the first part of which being the refrain (*responsum*), the second the shortened psalm verse.

The *responsum* is divided in two phrase members corresponding to the respective parts of the psalm tone structure:

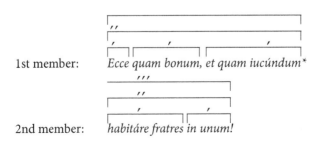

1st member: *Ecce quam bonum, et quam iucúndum**

2nd member: *habitáre fratres in unum!*

The first member is divided, in turn, in three incises, indicated by the quarter-bars, which coincide exactly with the three melodic-verbal units. The first incise (*Ecce*) is constructed on the dominant LA, with ornamentation of B-flat. The little *iubilus* of the accent forms two word-melodies, each of five notes. The cadence is simple, and remains on the degree of the dominant.

The second incise (*quam bonum*) preserves the accent on the dominant LA, while the composite cadence terminates to the lower register on MI.

In the third incise (*et quam iucundum*), two melodic-verbal accents are present: a secondary one on *quam* that once again reaches to the note LA, alternating to the ornamental SOL, before resting on the principal accent of *iu-cún-dum* on SOL and from there descending the interval of a fourth (SOL RE) to the final RE, repeating, in descending progression, the interval (LA MI) of the second incise. The ornamentation of the two accents makes use of the same melodic shape of five notes. The melodic apex of the entire phrase member is the accent of *Éc-ce*. The cadences of the incise are different under the rhythmic aspect: the first (*Éc-ce*: simple cadence) is a resolution in absolvency; the second (*bo-num*: a composite cadence) is a melodic extension with an *extensive* cadential articulation and with the last note in the role of pivot tone; the last (*iucun-dum*) is a simple cadence of resolution in dissolvency. This first phrase member calls for a single phrasing with the apex at the very beginning.

The second member (*habitare fratres in unum*) is divided in two incises by the half-bar of the VAT. The first incise rises to the strong tone DO, preceded by the first pre-tonic syllable on LA and the melodic gesture of the *bivirga*; the second begins on the tone LA, but with an extensive articulation that descends to SOL, the second note of the clivis. Also in this phrase member the beginning of the accent is preceded by a pre-tonic syllable on FA, in a descending melodic progression with the *incipit* of the preceding member: LA - DO, FA - LA. The composite final cadence of the second phrase member descends with the *torculus* to the sub-tonic scale degree DO; and from here it begins again with the accent *pes* FA - LA of the first word-melody, formed of six notes, to which follows, closely connected and in descending progression, the *pes quassus* of the accent type (FA - SOL) of the second word-melody of six notes. The melodic apex of the *responsum* of the present gradual is easily identified as corresponding to the text *habitare fratres in unum*.

The melodic construction of the *versus* bears the imprint of a psalm tone, with the following elements: *incipit, mediatio, reintonatio, flexa* and *terminatio*. Specifically:

The *incipit* (*Sicut unguentum*) is the accent *pes* RE - LA, the synthesis of the tonic-dominant, preceded by a prosthesis of two syllables. The *tenor* (= dominant) is LA. The *mediatio* (*in capite*), to the first full-bar, descends to FA. The *reintonatio* (*quod descendit*) is given by the accent *pes* LA - RE on *quod*. The *flexa* (*barbam*) after the *mediatio*, to the second full bar, descends to RE. The *terminatio*, to the end of the *versus*, concludes on RE.

First phrase: *Sic- ut   un- guén-tum   in   cá- pi- te,*

The text has received an ornamentation of a syllabic genre, with the *iubilus* placed on the final syllables. The *iubilus* of *unguentum* consists of six word-melodies, each of which is formed by the following number of notes: before the quarter-bar, five + five + four; after the quarter-bar, four + four + four. The word-melodies 2 and 3 are united to form a melodic incise with the accent note LA, and the word-melodies 5 and 6 form a melodic incise with the accent note SOL. These two melodic incises are connected by fragment 4.

The *iubilus* of the final syllable of *capite* contains two melodic-incises, of six notes each, not counting the doublings, and connected to one another by the note LA in between the repeated notes on DO.

Second phrase, before the flex:

quod   de- scén- dit   in   bar- bam,

The second phrase has two incises, divided by the quarter-bar, of the ornate genre within the text. In the first incise, the *pes* (LA - RE) on *quod* is a re-intonation; the little *iubilus* of the melodic-verbal accent on *de-scén-dit* rests on the note DO, in the role of the dominant; the notes of the *clivis* on the final syllable (SI - LA) constitute the melodic cadence of the *flexa*.

In the second incise, the *iubilus* of the accent, preceded by a pre-tonic syllable, begins on the note LA, and, by means of SOL and FA, descends progressively to the tone RE, the anticipation note of the final cadence, forming with this an extension of the redundant type. From the dominant LA, the *iubilus* descends to the tonic RE, forming four word-melodies, of four notes each, not counting the doublings. From the union of these word-melodies are obtained two melodic incises: the first of eight notes, from the word-melodies 1 and 2; the second incise of eight notes, from the word-melodies 3 and 4. The connection between the two incises is obtained with the ornamentation note SOL; moreover, the first note of every incise (LA and FA) carries the role of *initial articulation*.

Third phrase: *bar- bam   Aa- ron.*

The third phrase consists of two melodic-verbal units, with semi-ornate genre ornamentation of the text. The *iubilus* is outside of the text. The *incipit* begins on RE with the accent syllable of *bar-bam* which progresses to FA, with the ornamentation note SOL on the final syllable. With the accent syllable of *Aa-ron* it begins again from FA, rises to LA and from there descends immediately to FA.

The notes LA - LA - FA of the final syllable of the Hebrew word *Aaron* constitute the synthesis of the melodic accent and the cadence. From these, by means of the ornamentation on LA (first note of the *clivis*) it passes to SOL (second note of the *clivis*) from which flows the final *iubilus* of five word-melodies. The first three, of four notes each, form a descending melodic progression with a melodic extension of an octave; after the quarter-bar follow the last two word-melodies of five notes each, with the accents on FA, and the last word-melody with ornamentation of SOL to the accent, and the ornament of MI to the final. These two word-melodies trace an arch-form melodic design in ascending progression from the following notes:

$$\overset{\frown}{\text{DO - RE - FA - RE - DO}} \quad \overset{\frown}{\text{RE - FA - SOL - FA \ RE}}$$

There are twelve notes before the quarter-bar and twelve after the quarter-bar.

The first phrase of the *versus* is characterized by two phrasings, as correctly indicated by the half-bar, and with a cadential resolution in dissolvency.

The second phrase has only one punctuation of phrasing, at the quarter-bar. The final syllable of *descen-dit* forms a melodic cadence of resolution in dissolvency.

The third phrase is characterized by a single phrase, of which the melodic apex is the neume of the final syllable of *Aa-ron*. The quarter-bar should be removed, since it breaks the *iubilus* at its beginning point.

With regard to the rhythmic interpretation of the notes of articulation of the word-melodies, within the *iubilus*, the following synthesis may be given: notes marked with the vertical dash (|) have the role of "initial articulation"; notes marked with the plus sign (+) have the role of *pivot tone*, and notes with the asterisk (*) have the role of *resolution in absolvency*.

3. Interpretation

In Gregorian monody, text and melody form a perfect symbiosis, and this is exactly what the present treatise has attempted to demonstrate by means of the description of the properties of the accentuation of the Latin text, and by means of the analyses of some melodies, which, though following the laws proper to musical construction, adapt themselves as much as possible to the text, acquiring from them their oratorical properties and nuances.

In this adaptation, the various melodic genres of Gregorian chant, from the syllabic to the ornate, offer a vast creative synthesis, fruit of an experience and of an ability so fully developed that, in the presence of its creations and its sophistication, culturally prepared persons are amazed and fascinated. One could claim, without exaggeration, that the cultural and spiritual inheritance of the art of Gregorian composition, proper to the West, is of incomparable richness, and that up to this day has never been equaled.

To arrive at the goal of the interpretation of Gregorian chant, however, the study and understanding of it is not enough: what cannot be missing is the indispensable mediation in the person of the *interpreter*, who knows how to communicate to listeners those profound and religious sentiments of the texts with the genuine purity of the melodies from which they have taken form. The interpreter must allow the primary function of Gregorian chant to emerge, that is, to be prayer and proclamation, providing a vocal performance willing to be a *vehicle*, to communicate with the Divinity, and to communicate with men and women about the Divinity. This requires giving absolute preeminence to the inspired Word, which, after being welcomed and assimilated in its message, is exteriorly recreated in the musical interpretation of a colorful speech and of that melodic expressivity that does not attempt to impress the "senses," but rather to provoke religious thoughts and sentiments.

The *vocal expression* has its raison d'être in the text.

It must be tempered, discreet, calm: it must flow from a perfected musical intonation and from the purity of a natural voice so as to ingratiate itself into the souls of others; it must be conjoined with the descriptive, emotive and sometimes dramatic expressivity of the sung text. It has nothing to do with the angular and quantitatively more intense vocal color of the Roman and post-Gregorian periods, nor with that of the successive centuries up to our own day, with its associations strictly subordinated to musical language.

Melodic expressivity is a complex concept, which comprises:

1. The correct declamation of the text, the foundation of the rhythmic interpretation, is obtained, first, by assigning the appropriate autonomy to the word-rhythm and to the incise-rhythm. It is a fundamentally "verbal style," acquired through prolonged practice, and that knows only the boundaries of the "religious" maturity of the cantor.

2. The correct use of the melodic-verbal accent in the context of the greater phraseological accent. Every phrase contains one or more words that turn out to be more significant than others, and to which the composer has given a more elevated or more ornate melodic treatment. The interpreter must take care to confer the correct tension and relaxation to the melodic-verbal units in such a way that the phraseological accent does not gush forward suddenly or violently. The correct dynamic is one of the most efficacious means of making the *synthesis* of the greater rhythm.

The *rhythmic agogics*, or rather, the *rule* of rhythmic movement in general of the piece, is not separate from the dynamics. In other words, the movement of the melody is to be connected to its expressivity. The agogic connotation of the piece is, above all, drawn from the nature of the text and from the melodic genre of the composition, and is then put into relationship with the dynamic qualities that one intends to confer to the melody. Applied with discretion to the Gregorian melody, the agogic character constitutes the soul not only of the *greater rhythm*, but also of the melodic-verbal entities, and even of the plurisonic neumes. Otherwise, avoiding this essential component of rhythmic interpretation results inevitably in a cold and monotonous reading of Gregorian monody.

Finally, Gregorian interpretation cannot do without a certain *accent of pathos*, or in other words, of that vocal intonation in syntony with the various sentiments expressed by the texts and exalted by the melodies. Here we do not intend to speak of the modal construction of the pieces, understood as an expression of the diverse states of the soul, but rather of the affective participation of the interpreter, cantor or schola, who strive to translate into the voice the prayer, the supplication, the pain, the trust, the praise, and the thanksgiving of mankind. The pathos of the interpreter must maintain a natural and moderate connotation, not a romantic and theatrical one.

CHAPTER 5

SYMBIOSIS OF TEXT AND MELODY

1. Text and ornamentation

In the written tradition of Gregorian chant, significant evidence can be seen of musical forms that underwent procedures of ornamentation, not so much under the modal aspect as with regard to the melody. The musical forms particularly involved in this process belong to the primitive sources of liturgical chant, which find their origins in the recitative tones of the celebrant *orations*, in *psalmody*, as well as in the *litany* and in *free hymnody*.

A. Recitatives of the celebrant

The tones of the celebrant do not offer examples of rich ornamentation, since they could not deviate far from the *declamatory* melodic genre, having been composed exactly for the purpose of giving absolute preeminence to the text.

1. The tone of the *Preface*, in the three versions of the Missal. The *ferial* tone, using only monosonic neumes; the *solemn* tone, with cadences for punctuation in semi-ornate phrasing; finally, the *sollemnior* tone, with melodies of semi-ornate genre, of more recent elaboration with respect to the preceding tones.

ex. 5.1

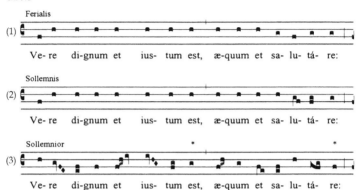

Ferialis

(1) Ve- re   di-gnum et   ius- tum est,   æ-quum et sa- lu- tá- re:

Sollemnis

(2) Ve- re   di-gnum et   ius- tum est,   æ-quum et sa- lu- tá- re:

Sollemnior   *   *

(3) Ve- re   di-gnum et   ius- tum est,   æ-quum et sa- lu- tá- re:

(1) Te qui- dem, Dó-mi- ne,   om-ni   témpo- re,   sed in hoc [...]

(2) Te qui- dem, Dó-mi- ne,   om-ni   témpo- re,   sed in hoc [...]

(3) Te qui- dem, Dó-mi- ne,   om-ni   témpo- re,   sed in hoc [...]

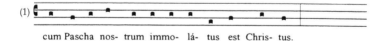

(1) cum Pascha nos- trum immo- lá- tus est Chris- tus.

(2) cum Pascha nos- trum immo- lá- tus est Chris- tus.

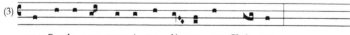

(3) cum Pascha nos- trum immo- lá- tus est Chris- tus.

2. *The Lord's Prayer*, in the *ferial* tone and the *festive* tone. The latter has the melodic accent on FA with a semi-ornate melodic cadence of the phrases.

ex. 5.2

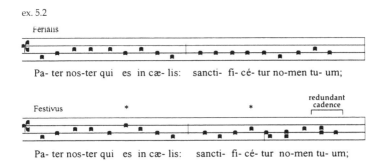

B. *Psalmody*
Tone of RE

The liturgical-musical forms belonging both to the repertory of the psalmist and to that of the schola have preserved an extended documentation of the tone of RE.

From the repertory of the psalmist

1. The versicle of Psalm 140, in the textual version of *Vespertina oratio* and of the *Dirigatur*, is all that the written tradition preserved of the psalmody *in directum*,[1] which preceded the advent of the schola. In this psalmody, the *iubilus* is not within the text, the melodic shape of *Dirigatur* is more elaborate, and the accent of the *iubilus* rises to FA, beyond the bounds of pentatonicism (cf. ex. 3.32 and ex. 3.33 on pp. 104 and 105).

2. In the verses of *Homo pacis meæ* from the season of Lent and from *Deus in adiutorium* (*et in sæcula*), the *iubilus* of *Vespertina oratio* enters into the midst of the text with syllabic ornamentation

---

1. One of the earliest documented forms of Psalmody for the Office and the Mass is psalmody *in directum*, in which the verses of the psalm are chanted without any type of refrain.

in the first case, and semi-ornate ornamentation in the second. In this melodic version the final descends to DO.

ex. 5.3

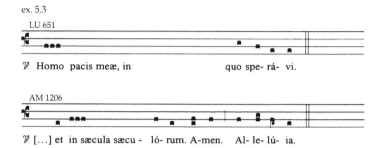

3. The "response" part of the Brief Responsories was modeled after the melody of the *iubilus* of the psalmody *in directum*. The part for the soloist (Vs) also received ample ornamentation.

ex. 5.4

4. The "response" of the responsorial psalmody later became the antiphons with different ornamentation.

ex. 5.5

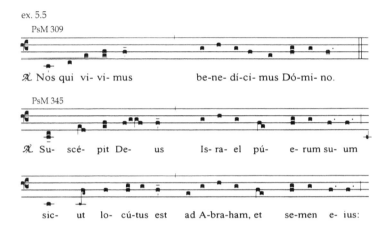

5. The adding of texts to the *iubilus* of the versicle *Vespertina oratio* brought about the formation of the syllabic genre tone of RE.

ex. 5.6

6. GREG elaborated two other different ornamentations of the tone of RE for the Invitatory Psalm 94. In the melodic version B of ex. 5.7, the tenor climbs one scale degree to MI (written as LA in the LH) and the final cadence is in a semi-ornate melodic genre.

ex. 5.7 (1) LH 165

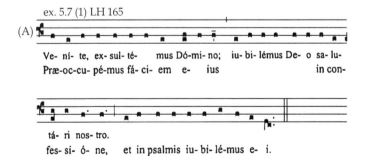

ex. 5.7 (2) LH 16

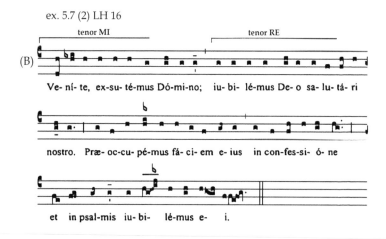

7. The *iubilus* of the versicle *Dirigatur* (ex. 3.31) moves within the body of the text to form ornate cadences of four and five syllables.

From the repertory of the schola

ex. 5.8

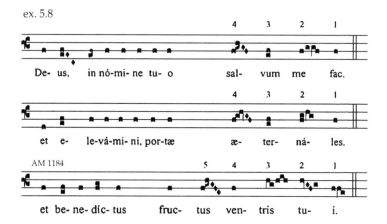

8. The Tracts of Mode II represent a more complex elaboration created at the very source of the tone of RE. Notice especially the composition of the *incipit* and the final cadence that recover in

the *terminatio* the small *iubilus* of the versicle *Vespertina oratio* (ex. 3.32 on p. 104).

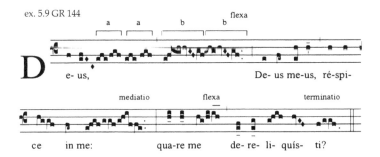

ex. 5.9 GR 144

9. The verses of the Graduals of Mode II, which originate in the tone of RE, have an evolved elaboration of the Tone, with the tenor on RE and the final cadence on LA.

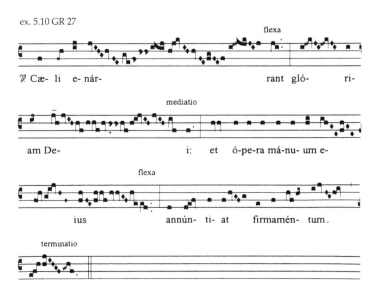

ex. 5.10 GR 27

Tone of MI[2]

10. Tone I, in the syllabic genre, received the imprint of the solemn version of the versicle *Deus, in adiutorium.*

ex. 5.11

℣ De- us, in adiutórium me- um in- tén- de.

11. The Christmas Ant. *Hodie Christus natus est* is composed with the material of the semi-ornate Tone I.

ex. 5.12 AM 249

℟ Hó-di- e   Chris-   tus na- tus est: ho- di- e [...]

hó-di- e   in ter-ra   ca-nunt An-ge- li

læ-tán- tur Archán-ge- li:

2. The tones of DO (C), RE (D), and MI (E) are the "archaic modes," first theorized by Dom Jean Claire, OSB, in a series of articles in 1962–1975, and that first appeared in chant books in the GS, in the chant books of Solesmes with the PsM, and the LH, and were extensively presented in Alberto Turco, *Il Canto Gregoriano*, vol. 2, Toni e Modi (Rome: Edizioni Torre d'Orfeo, 1996[3]). English translation by Stefano Concordia, *Gregorian Chant: Tones and Modes* (Rome: Edizioni Torre d'Orfeo, 2003).

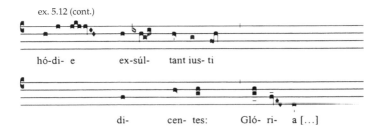

ex. 5.12 (cont.)

hó-di- e   ex-súl-   tant ius- ti

di-   cen- tes: Gló- ri-   a [...]

Tone of DO

12. The ornamentation of the simple and solemn Easter tones, from the semi-ornate to the ornate genre, with the greater melodic extension from a fifth to that of a seventh.

ex. 5.13

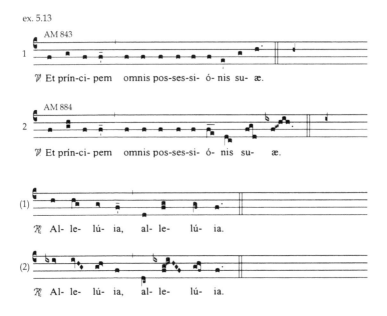

AM 843

1

℣ Et prín-ci- pem   omnis pos-ses-si- ó- nis su-   æ.

AM 884

2

℣ Et prín-ci- pem   omnis pos-ses-si- ó- nis su-   æ.

(1)

℟ Al- le- lú- ia,   al- le- lú- ia.

(2)

℟ Al- le- lú- ia,   al- le- lú- ia.

13. The ornamentation of the antiphons *Domine, refugium*, *Benedictus Dominus*, and *Benedictus Deus*, derives from the tone of DO responsorial psalmody, with the various adaptations of the melody to the literary texts (cf. p. 231 ex. A.41).

The ornamentation of the antiphon *Crucifixus*, particularly in the modal solidity of its final cadence, derives from the melodic shape of the tone of DO syllabic genre. (cf. p. 232 ex. A.42.)

C. The Litany

The *Kyrie eleison* is the most ancient form of Litany. In the Roman liturgy, since the time of Pope Gregory the Great (d. 604), the *Kyrie* is placed at the beginning of the Mass, alternated with *Christe eleison*. In other liturgies, for instance in the Ambrosian rite, it is repeated several times in the celebration. Without providing analyses of the melodies of the *Kyrie*, some examples are offered of the various ornamentations of the same formula.

1. The ornamentation of the litanical formula *Kyrie eleison* of the Mode of MI and its modal development. The accent and the dominant are raised to SOL in the *Christe eleison*, and the accent of the last *Kyrie* is raised to LA (cf. ex. A.43 p. 233).

2. The last *Kyrie* of KR XII is obtained by the juxtaposition of two melodic formulas: one from the *Kyrie* and one from *eleison* of the *Christe*.

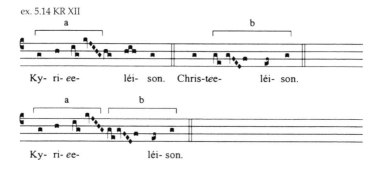

ex. 5.14 KR XII

Ky- ri- ee-   léi- son.   Chris-tee-   léi- son.

Ky- ri- ee-   léi- son.

3. From the ornamentation on FA the melody ascends to SOL in the *Christe*, and develops the ornamentation of the accent. The last *Kyrie* rises to the dominant LA using the preceding formulas.

ex. 5.15 KR XIII

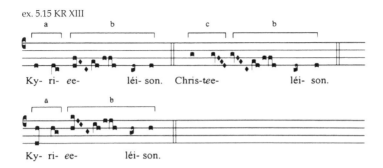

4. The following example illustrates the development of the ornamentation from *Kyrie X* (*Alma Pater*) to *Kyrie IX* (*Cum jubilo*).

ex. 5.16

ex. 5.16 (cont.)

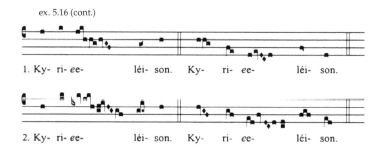

1. Ky- ri- ee-   léi- son.   Ky-   ri- ee-   léi-   son.

2. Ky- ri- ee-   léi- son.   Ky-   ri- ee-   léi-   son.

D. Ancient hymnody

Hymnody is a musical form analogous to psalmody and present from the origins of liturgical chant. It consists in poetic compositions whose textual content is *praise*. In his commentary of Psalm 72, St. Augustine writes, "If it treats of praise and if this praise is not addressed to God, it is not a hymn. If it is of praise, and praise of God, but it is not sung, it is not a hymn. For it to be a hymn, there must these three: praise, God, and song."[3]

There is no allusion to the form of the literary text in this testimonial. Like the Psalms, the texts of ancient hymns are not strophic, nor metrical, as are the hymns in the modern sense, but they are in a more or less cadenced prose, with the result that their melodic attire is comparable to that of primitive psalmody: a recitation tone and a *iubilus* on the final syllable of a word at the end of a phrase member. Emblematic of ancient hymnody are the *Gloria in excelsis* and the *Te Deum*.

1. The following is a comparison of the ornamentation of the *Gloria in excelsis* in the tone of RE in two different liturgical traditions, the Spanish and the Gregorian. A third melodic version, from the Ambrosian repertory of the thirteenth-fourteenth centuries, can be considered a simplification of the Gregorian *Gloria XI* (Cf. ex. A.44 at p. 234).

---

3. Cf. St. Augustine, *Ennarratio in Psalmum 72, I*: "Hymni sunt cantus continentes laudem Dei; si sit laus et non sit Dei, non est hymnus. Si sit laus Dei et non cantetur non est hymnus. Oportet, ut sit hymnus, habeat hæc tria: et laudem, et Dei, et canticum."

2. The *Te Deum* and its ornamentation are presented in the three Gregorian melodic versions, and the Ambrosian version (Cf. ex. A.45 pp. 236–237).

In the introductory part, (*A*) versions 2, 3, and 4 are more ornate and with a melodic-verbal accent on DO. In version 4 the accent of DO remains in the second introductory part (*B*).

Phrase member *C* shifts the accentuation to SI, with the melodic accent on DO in versions 1 and 3, and the reciting tone to DO in versions 2, 4, and 5.

Phrase member *D* repeats the ornamentation of *B*.

Finally, the variety of ornamentation on the word *Sanctus* (*D*) should be observed.

3. A comparison of the ornamentation of the *Credo* follows, in the Ambrosian, Spanish, and Gregorian traditions.

In MIL, it is built upon the tone of RE (transposed to SOL), repeating the same cadence for each phrase member of the text.

In HISP, the reciting tone of the first part climbs to MI (written as LA), with the ornamentation on FA (= B-flat). The provisional cadence of the penultimate phrase member (in semi-ornate genre, with the function of melodic connection) is built on SI (written as MI). The concluding formula begins with melodic accent on MI (=LA), with the ornamentation of FA (= B-flat), to conclude on RE (=SOL).

In GREG, *Credo I* is comparable, in composition and in ornamentation, to the version of HISP. *Credo II*, on the other hand, though it does not have the ornamentation of B-flat, does have an evolved modality compared to that of the preceding versions. It has two cadences to melodic degrees that differ from the original reciting tone, RE (written as SOL): the intermediate cadence of the first incise (*omnipotentem*) on DO (= FA), and the final cadence on B-natural (= MI).

2. Text and composition

The Gregorian melody is founded on the primary element of the literary text. It follows the natural line of the word, projected by the rhythmic synthesis of the phrasing within the wider context that includes the incise and the phrase. Within the symbiosis of text and music, Gregorian monody contains various melodic elements and episodes, especially in the ornamentation of the text, which go beyond compositional technique, through the use of imitation, progression, modal development, or by other means. These elements are used by the Gregorian compositional art not so much for aesthetic purposes, but rather for a sublimation, through sound, of the literary text, in relation to its primary quality of prayer and announcement of a mystery.

A. *The syllable*

The spiritual content of the sung text can be better expressed when certain syllables of the text are presented with the same neume. In the Co. *Dominus firmamentum*, for instance, the accent syllables of certain key words are voiced by the same neume: cf. *firmamentum, liberator, adiutor*.

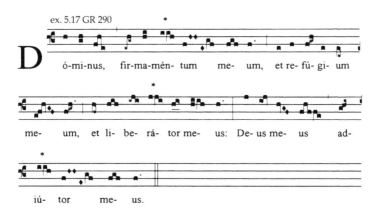

(*The Lord is my rock, my fortress, and my deliverer; / my God is my saving strength*) Roman Missal, Ps 18(17):3

In the following example, the final syllables of a word receive the same melodic ornamentation in a suspensive type of cadence to give continuity to the phrasing within the piece. The composer uses the accent neume of an inverted redundant cadence formula on MI three times.

([*The Lord said to Peter:*] *When you were young, you fastened your own belt and walked where you would; but when you are old, you will stretch out your hands, and another will fasten your belt for you and carry you where you do not wish to go. [This he said to show by what death he was to glorify God.]*) John 21:18-19

Sometimes, the composer seems almost unable to free himself from the melodic line drawn by an accent neume, as if to constitute a leitmotif of the piece. In the In. *Invocabit me*, this can be observed in the accent neume of the words *invocabit, ego, eripiam,* and *glorificabit,* and in the cadences of sentences and phrase members at *a* and *b*.

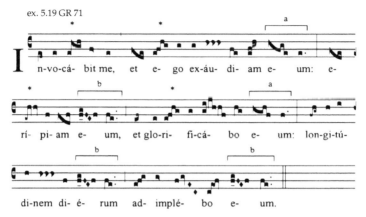

ex. 5.19 GR 71

n-vo-cá- bit me, et e- go ex-áu- di- am e- um: e-

rí- pi- am e- um, et glo-ri- fi-cá- bo e- um: lon-gi-tú-

di-nem di- é- rum ad- implé- bo e- um.

(When he calls on me, I will answer him; / I will deliver him and give him glory, / I will grant him length of days.) Roman Missal, Ps 91(90):15-16

In the In. *Spiritus Domini,* syllables and words have the same neumes:

a. *terra-rum* | *et hoc* | *quod con-tinet*

b. *om-nia* | *scien-tiam*

c. *orbem* | *habet*

In addition, the finals of the *alleluias* are constructed on the melody tones of the first phrase.

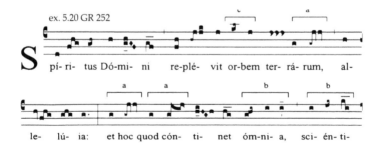

ex. 5.20 GR 252

pí- ri- tus Dó-mi- ni   re-plé- vit or-bem ter- rá- rum,   al-

le- lú- ia: et hoc quod cón- ti- net   óm-ni- a,   sci- én- ti-

ex. 5.20 (cont.)

am   ha-bet vo- cis, al- le- lú- ia, al- le- lú- ia, al-

le-   lú- ia.

(The Spirit of the Lord has filled the whole world / and that which contains all things / understands what is said, alleluia.) Roman Missal, Wis 1:7

In the Co. *Domine memorabor,* four syllables are ornamented with the identical neume: *iusti-ti-æ, so-li-us, se-ni-um, de-re-linquas.*

ex. 5.21 GR 332

Dó- mi- ne, me-mo- rá- bor ius-tí- ti- æ tu- æ so-

lí-   us: De- us do- cu- ís- ti me a iu-ven-tú- te me- a,

et us- que in se-néc- tam et sé- ni- um, De- us, ne de-

re-   línquas me.

(I will praise your righteousness, yours alone. O God from my youth you have taught me, and I still proclaim your wondrous deeds. So even to old age and grey hairs, O God, do not forsake me.) Ps 71:17-18

B. The word

The Gregorian composition will, at times, apply a particular ornamentation to a significant word. At the beginning of a piece, the first one or two words receive an ornamentation that is clearly detached from the following melodic context, as if to function as a type of "overture."

From the In. *Lex Domini*:

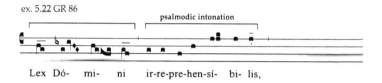

ex. 5.22 GR 86

Lex Dó- mi- ni   ir-re-pre-hen-sí- bi- lis,

From the In. *Deus in nomine tuo*:

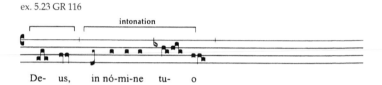

ex. 5.23 GR 116

De- us,   in nó-mi-ne   tu-   o

From the Tr. *Deus, Deus meus*:

ex. 5.24 GR 144

De- us   De- us me- us,

In the Co. *Qui manducat*, the possessive pronouns *meam/meum*, are underlined by a distinctive ornamentation, while the pronoun *me* is positioned at the melodic apex. In this text, the realistic vocabulary of "eating and drinking" refers to the sacrament of the Last Supper of the Lord, and wants to signify that consuming the eucharistic bread is the true manner of participation in the life of Jesus. The accent on the word *dícit* receives a flowering of notes that strikingly distinguishes it from the rest of the piece. The melodic expansion of *dicit* by the composer is an explicit allusion to the dissent produced by the aforementioned words of Jesus in the hearts of the listeners and, in the liturgical contextualization, an invitation to give thanks to the Lord for the gift of the Eucharist.

(Whoever eats my flesh and drinks my blood / remains in me and I in him, says the Lord.) Roman Missal, John 6:57

In the Co. *Quinque prudentes virgines*, the verbs *clamor* and *exite* sing at the apex of the piece and with intense expressivity, especially with the first verb, signifying the sudden arrival of the spouse in the heart of the night and the invitation to enter with him into the wedding chamber. Moreover, the great melisma on the word *Christo* is extracted from the word *mortem* (died) in the Gr. *Christus factus est* (GT 148). The spouse, for whom the virgins had been awaiting, is the Christ condemned to death. Accordingly, the text is sung at the celebrations in honor of the virgin martyrs.

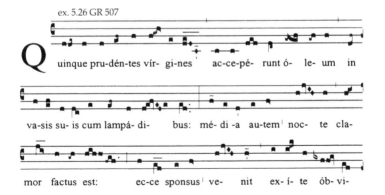

ex. 5.26 (cont.)

am Chris-   to   Dó-mi- no.

(The five wise virgins took their lamps with the oil. At midnight a cry was heard: "Behold, the Spouse is coming! Go and meet Christ, your Lord!") Cf. Matt 25:4, 6

One can find the repetition of the same melody on several words of the same importance and belonging to the same conceptual unit: cf. in the In. *In medio Ecclesiæ*, the words *sapientiæ, et intellectus.*

ex. 5.27 GR 493

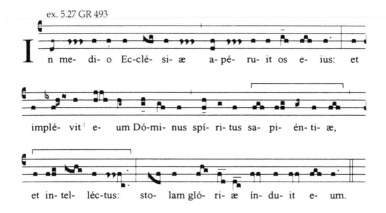

n me-   di- o Ec-clé- si- æ   a- pé- ru- it os   e-   ius: et

implé- vit ¹ e-   um Dó-mi- nus spí- ri- tus sa- pi-   én- ti- æ,

et in- tel-   léc-tus: sto- lam gló- ri- æ ín- du- it   e-   um.

(In the midst of the Church he opened his mouth, / and the Lord filled him with the spirit of wisdom and understanding / and clothed him in a robe of glory.) Roman Missal, cf. Sir 15:5

A significant word within a liturgical season (Advent) is present in two separate pieces and receives the identical melody: cf. the word *salutare* in the Co. *Revelabitur* and *Viderunt omnes.*

ex. 5.28 GR 41 & 50

sa- lu- tá-   re De-   i   nos- tri.

The composer resorts to repetition of the same formula several times in the *Co. Domine memorabor*, previously cited (cf. ex. 5.21). Here, four key words, all but the last with four syllables each, receive the same formula: *iustitiæ*, *in senectam*, *senium*, and *solius*.

C. The phrase member

Textual repetitions of phrase members in the verses of the Of. *Vir erat* can be observed. It is highly probable that the numerous repetitions contained in this Offertory constitute an addendum of chants, due to the continuation of the rite of the presentation of the gifts.

ex. 5.29 OF 122

ex. 5.29 (cont.)

nam   appende-réntur   peccá-ta   me-   a :

ú- ti- nam   appende-réntur

peccá- ta me-   a, qui-bus   i-   ram

mé-ru-   i, qui- bus   i- ram   mé-ru-   i,

et ca-lá- mi- tas   et ca- lá-   mi- tas

et ca-lá- mi- tas,   quam pá-   ti-   or, et grá- vi- or

appa-   ré-   ret. ℣. 2. Quae est e- nim, quae

est   e- nim,   quae est e-nim forti-túdo me-

a,   ut sustí- ne- am?   Aut quis fi-nis me- us,   ut pa-

ti- énter a-   gam? Aut fi-nis me- us,   ut pa- ti- én-

ter a-   gam? ℣. 3. Numquid forti- tú-   do lá-

ex. 5.29 (cont.)

(*There was a man in the land whose name was Job, a blameless, righteous and God-fearing man. Satan asked to tempt him, and the Lord gave him power over his possessions and his body; and so he destroyed what he owned and his children, and he afflicted his flesh with horrible sores.*
Translation: Dr. Kate Helsen, London, Ontario, Canada, The Gregorian Repertory, https://gregorien.info/chant/id/8670/0/en

V.1. Oh, if you would measure the weight of my sins, for which I have deserved this punishment, and the pain that are the greatest—of the sands of the sea.
V.2. How to find the strength to persevere? What sense is there to be patient?

V.3. Do I have the compactness of a boulder? Has my flesh the firmness of bronze?
V.4. Because my eyes will never see the good again.)

Repetitions of phrase members can be found in these other offertories:
Iubilate Deo omnis terra (cf. ex. A.10 p. 197)
Iubilate Deo universa terra (GR 227)
Precatus est Moyses (GR 317)
Gloriabuntur V.2. Quoniam ad te orabo (OF 136)

D. *The phrase and the complete sentence*

The art of Gregorian composition also addresses the theme of dramatization in the melody, especially with narrative and prophetic biblical texts. The text of the Co. *Dicit Dominus: Implete hydrias aqua* develops on three different melodic ranges, each of which is attributed to a character from the Gospel story:

• Medium melodic range for the "historian": *Dicit Dominus*; *Cum gustasset architriclino aquam vinum factam, dicit sponso*; *Hoc signum fecit Iesus primum coram discipulis suis.*

• Low melodic range for Christ: *Implete hydrias aqua et ferte architriclinus.*

• Acute melodic range for a "character" in general: *Servasti vinum bonum usque adhuc.*

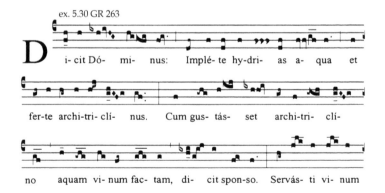

ex. 5.30 GR 263
Di- cit Dó- mi- nus: Implé- te hy-dri- as a- qua et
fer-te archi-tri- clí- nus. Cum gus- tás- set archi-tri- clí-
no   aquam vi- num fac- tam, di- cit spon-so. Servás- ti vi- num

ex. 5.30 (cont.)

bo- num us- que ad-huc. Hoc signum fe- cit Ie-sus pri-mum co-ram

di-scí- pu- lis su- is.

(Jesus said to them, "Fill the jars with water" . . . and take it to the stew-
ard of the feast." . . . When the steward of the feast tasted the water now
become wine, and did not know where it had come from . . . he called
the bridegroom and said to him, . . . "You have kept the good wine until
now." This, the first of his signs, Jesus did at Cana in Galilee in the presence
of his disciples.) John 2:7, 8, 9 and 10-11

This melodic dramatization, common to that of the story of the
Passion of the Lord, is a motivated choice of the composer, who
actually wants to connect the story of the first miracle performed
by the Lord with that of his Passion: two facts that are found, respectively, at the beginning and at the end of the Gospel of St. John.

The words of the Lord are usually sung in the lower melodic
range:

Co. *In splendoribus* (GR 44,4) text of Psalm 109:3

Co. *Venite post me* (GR 267) Gospel text of Matthew 4:19-20

Co. *Amen dico vobis: quod vos* (GR 436,2) Gospel text of Matthew
19:28

Co. *Simon Ioannis* (GR 574,4) Gospel text of John 21:15, 17

Finally, texts of a prophetic nature are also highlighted in the
Gregorian composition. For example, the text of the Ant. *Scriptum*
est enim percutiam contains the announcement of the future resur-
rection of Christ. The words of this announcement represent the
melodic apex of entire antiphon.

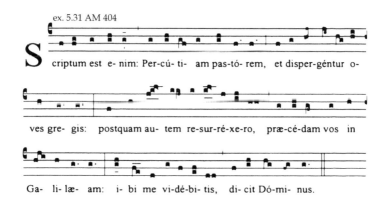

ex. 5.31 AM 404

S criptum est e- nim: Per-cú- ti- am pas-tó- rem,   et disper-géntur o-

ves gre- gis: postquam au- tem re-sur-ré-xe-ro,   præ-cé-dam vos   in

Ga- li- læ- am: i- bi me vi-dé-bi- tis,   di- cit Dó-mi- nus.

(For it is written . . . I will strike the shepherd and the sheep of the flock will be scattered. But after I am raised up, I will go before you to Galilee, says the Lord.) Matt 26:31-32

APPENDIX

Manuscript illustrations, selection of chants, graphic tables

ex. A.1 GR 15

A
d te le-vá- vi á- nimam me- am: De- us me- us

in te confí- do non e- ru- bés- cam: ne-que ir-rí- de-

ant me i-ni-mí- ci me- i: ét- e- nim u- ni-vér- si qui teex-

spéc- tant, non confun- dén- tur. *Ps.* Vi- as tu- as, Dó-mi-ne, de-

monstra mi- hi: et sé-mi-tas tu- as do- ce me.

ex. A.2 GR 117

C ircumdedé-runt me gémi-tus mor-tis, do-ló- res infér-ni cir-

cum- de- dé- runt me: et in tri- bu-la- ti- ó- ne me- a

invo- cá- vi Dó- mi-num, et ex- au-dí- vit de templo sancto

su- o vo- cem me- am. *Ps.* Dí- ligam te, Dómi-ne, vir-

tus me-a: Dó-minus firmaméntum me- um, et re-fú-gi- um me- um.

ex. A.3 GR 103

M i- se-ré-re mi-hi, Dómi- ne, quó- ni- am in- fír-

mus sum: sa-na me, Dómi- ne. ℣ Contur-

bá- ta sunt óm- ni-

a os-sa me- a: et á- nima me- a

tur-bá- ta est ' val-de.

ex. A.4 GR 196

R e-sur- ré-xi et adhuc tecum sum, al- le- lú- ia:

po- su- ís- ti su- per me ma- num tu- am, al- le- lú- ia:

mi-rá- bi- lis fac- ta est sci- én- ti- a tu- a, al-le- lú-

ia, al- le- lú- ia. *Ps.* Dó- mi- ne, pro- bás- ti me et

cogno-vís- ti me: tu cogno-vís- ti ses-si- ó- nem me- am, et re- sur-

rec- ti- ó- nem me- am.

ex. A.5 GR 377

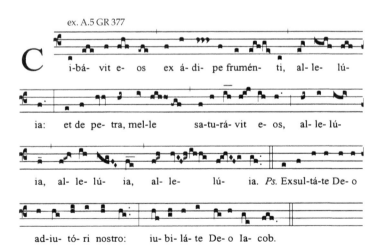

C i-bá- vit e- os ex á- di- pe frumén- ti, al- le- lú-

ia: et de pe- tra, mel-le sa-tu-rá- vit e- os, al- le- lú-

ia, al- le- lú- ia, al- le- lú- ia. *Ps.* Exsul-tá-te De- o

ad-iu- tó- ri nostro: iu- bi- lá- te De- o Ia- cob.

ex. A.6 GR 256

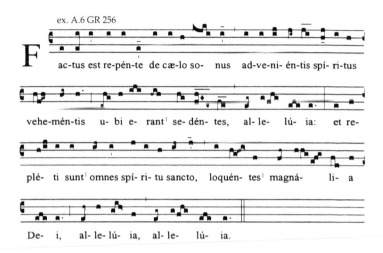

vehe-mén-tis   u- bi e- rant[|] se- dén- tes,   al- le-   lú- ia: et re-

plé- ti sunt[|] omnes spí- ri- tu sancto,   loquén- tes[|] magná-   li- a

De- i,   al- le- lú- ia,   al- le-   lú- ia.

ex. A.7

(1) PsM 340

Be- ne- díc- tus Dó- mi- nus De- us me- us.

(2) PsM 191

Be- ne- di- xís- ti,   Dó- mi- ne,   ter- ram tu- am.

(3) PsM 103

E- ruc-tá- vit   cor me-   um ver-bum bo- num.

(4) PsM 91

Re- vé- la   Dó- mi- no   vi- am tu- am.

ex. A.7 (cont.)

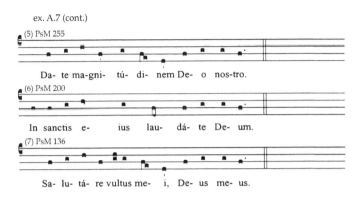

(5) PsM 255

Da- te ma-gni- tú- di- nem De- o nos-tro.

(6) PsM 200

In sanctis e- ius lau- dá- te De- um.

(7) PsM 136

Sa- lu- tá- re vultus me- i, De- us me- us.

ex. A.8

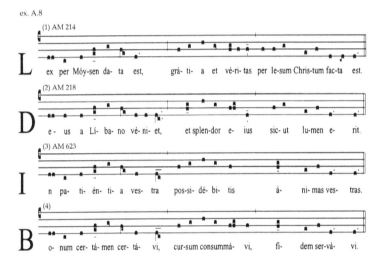

(1) AM 214

L ex per Móy-sen da- ta est, grá- ti- a et vé-ri- tas per Ie-sum Chris-tum fac-ta est.

(2) AM 218

D e- us a Lí- ba- no vé- ni- et, et splen-dor e- ius sic- ut lu-men e- rit.

(3) AM 623

I n pa- ti- én- ti- a ves- tra pos-si- dé- bi- tis á- ni- mas ves- tras.

(4)

B o- num cer- tá- men cer- tá- vi, cur-sum consummá- vi, fi- dem ser-vá- vi.

ex. A.9 GR 251

U l- ti- mo fes- ti- vi- tá- tis di-   e   di-cé-bat Ie-sus:

Qui in me cre-   dit,   flúmi-na de ventre e- ius flu- ent a-

quæ vi- væ.   Hoc au-tem di- xit de Spí- ri- tu, quem ac-cep-tú- ri e-

rant cre-dén-tes   in   e-   um,   al- le- lú-   ia,   al-

le-   lú-   ia.

Description:

In this Communion Antiphon there are two phrases in *tritus*: *credentes in eum,* and the final *alleluia.* The rest is entirely in *protus,* but written in, and with the final cadence on, LA (=RE). Within the composition of *protus,* on the dominant DO (= FA) there are cadential formulas of *tritus*: *die, in me credit,* and the first *alleluia.* Moreover, the incipit (*ultimo*) is formed by the modal cell of the archaic mode of RE: LA-SOL-LA-SOL-MI-MI (= RE-DO-RE-DO-LA-LA). What follows then is the centonized formula of *protus-deuterus,* with the last note having slid up to DO: MI-RE-SOL-LA-SI -DO (= RE-DO-FA-SOL-LA-SI-flat).

ex. A.10 GR 259

I u- bi- lá- te De- o om-nis ter-

ra: iu-bi- lá-

te De- o om- nis ter-

ra, ser-ví- te Dó- mi- no in læ-

tí- ti- a: in-trá- te in con-spéc-tu e- ius in

ex-sul-ta- ti- ó- ne, qui- a Dó- mi- nus ip- se

est De- us

ex. A.11

MODŒTIENSIS	RHENAUGIENSIS	BLANDINIENSIS
	AD COM. In splendoribus sanctorum ex utero ante luciferum genui te.	AD COM. In splendoribus sanctorum ex utero ante luciferum genui te. PSALM. Dixit Dominus Domino meo. AD REPET. Tecum principium.
MANE PRIMA.	ITEM AD MISSAM MANE PRIMA IN DIE NATALIS DOMINI.	MANE PRIMA AD SANCTAM ANASTASIAM.
	ANT. Lux folgebit hodie super nos quia natus est nobis Dominus & vocabitur (pag. 4) Admirabilis Deus Pater futuri seculi cujus regni non erit finis. PSALM. Dominus regnavit.	ANT. Lux fulgebit hodie super nos quia natus est nobis Dominus & vocabitur Admirabilis Deus Princeps pacis Pater futuri seculi cujus regni non erit finis. PSALM. Dominus regnavit decore.
RESP. GRAD. Benedictus qui venit in nomine Domini Deus Dominus et inluxit nobis. ℣. A Domino factum est et est mirabile in oculis nostris.	GRAD. Benedictus qui venit in nomine Domini Deus Dominus & inluxit nobis.℣. A Domino factum est & est mirabile in oculis nostris.	RESP. GRAD. Benedictus qui venit in nomine Domini Deus Dominus & inluxit nobis. ℣. A Domino factum est & est mirabile in oculis nostris.
ALL. Dominus regnavit decorem induit.	ALL. Dominus regnavit decorem induit induit Dominus fortitudinem & precinxit se virtutem.	ALL. Dominus regnavit decorem.
	OFF. Deus enim firmavit orbem terre qui non commovebitur parata sedis tua Deus ex tunc a seculo tu es ¹.	OFF. Deus enim firmavit orbem terre qui non commovebitur parata sedis tua Deus ex tunc a seculo tu es. ℣. [I.] Dominus regnavit decorem. ℣. II. Mirabilis in altis Dominus.
	AD COM. Exulta filia Sion lauda filia Hierusalem ecce Rex tuus venit jus[tus] & Salvator mundi.	AD COM. Exsulta //// Sion lauda filia Hierusalem ecce Rex tuus vinit justus & Salvator mundi. PSALM. ut supra ¹.
IN DIE NATALIS DOMINI.	VIII KALENDAS JANUARIAS NATALE DOMINI AD MISSAM IN DIAE AD SANCTUM PETRUM.	DIE NATALIS DOMINI STATIO AD SANCTUM PETRUM.
	ANT. Puer natus est nobis & filius datus est nobis cujus imperium super humerum ejus & vocabitur nomen ejus magni consilii Angelus. PSALM. Cantate Domino canticum.	ANT. Puer natus est nobis & filius datus est nobis cujus imperium super humerum ejus & vocabitur nomen ejus magni consilii Angelus. PSALM. Cantate Domino. II.
RESP. GRAD. Viderunt omnes fines terre salutare Dei nostri jubilate Deo omnis terra. ℣. Notum fecit Dominus salutare suum ante conspectu gentium revelabit justitiam suam.	GRAD. Viderunt omnes fines terre salutare Dei nostri jubilate ² Deo omnis terra. ℣. Notum fecit Dominus salutare suum conspectu gentium revelabit justiciam suam.	RESP. GRAD. Viderunt omnes fines terre salutare Dei nostri jubilate Deo omnis terra. ℣. Notum fecit Dominus salutare suum ante conspectu gentium revelabit justiciam suam.
	(1) ms. : ēē. (2) ms : jubilato.	(1) ms. : suprā.

ex. A.11 (cont.)

COMPENDIENSIS	(K) CORBIENSIS	SILVANECTENSIS
COM. In splendoribus sanctorum ex utero ante luciferum genui te.	COM. In splendoribus sanctorum ex utero ante luciferum genui te. *PSALM.* Dixit Dominus.	COM. In splendoribus sanctorum. PSALM. Dixi Dominus Domino meo. AD RE-PET. Tecum principium.
MANE PRIMA STATIO AD SANCTAM ANASTASIAM.	IN VIGILIA MANE PRIMA STATIO AD SANCTAM ANASTASIAM. [CAP.] X.	IN VIGILIA MANE PRIMA. STATIO AD HIERUSALEM.
ANT. Lux fulgebit hodie super nos quia natus est nobis Dominus et vocabitur Admirabilis Deus Princeps pacis Pater futuri saeculi cujus regni non erit finis. PSALM. Dominus regnavit decore. AD REPET. Parata sedes. RESP. GRAD. Benedictus qui venit in nomine Domini Deus Dominus et inluxit nobis. ℣. A Domino factum est et est mirabile in oculis nostris.	ANT. (Plagis Tetrardi.) Lux fulgebit hodie super nos quia natus est nobis Dominus et vocabitur Admirabilis Deus Princeps pacis Pater futuri saeculi cujus regni non erit finis. PSALM. Dominus regnavit decorem. RESP. GRAD. Benedictus qui venit in nomine Domini Deus Dominus & inluxit nobis. (Iol. 4) ℣. A Domino factum est & est mirabile in oculis nostris.	[ANT.] Lux fulgebit hodie super nos. PSALM. Dominus regnavit .I. AD RE-PET. Parata sedes tua. RESP. GRAD. Benedictus qui venit. ℣. A Domino factum est.
ALL. Dominus regnavit decore induit induit Dominus fortitudinem et praecinxit se virtute. OFF. Deus enim firmavit orbem terrae qui non commovebitur parata sedes tua Deus ex tunc a saeculo tu es. ℣.I. Dominus regnavit decore induit induit Dominus fortitudinem et precinxit se virtute. ex tunc. (Iol. 4ᵛ) ℣. II. Mirabilis in excelsis Dominus testimonia tua credibilia facta sunt nimis domum tuam decet sancta Domine in longitudine dierum. COM. Exulta filia Sion lauda filia Hierusalem ecce rex tuus venit sanctus et Salvator mundi. PSALM. ut supra.	ALL. Dominus regnavit decorem induit induit Dominus fortitudinem & precinxit se virtute. OFF. Deus enim firmavit orbem terrae qui non commovebitur parata sedes tua Deus ex tunc a saeculo tu es. COM. (Plagis Deuteri.) Exulta filia Sion lauda filia Hierusalem ecce Rex tuus venit sanctus & Salvator mundi.	ALL. Dominus regnavit decore. OFF. Deus enim firmavit. ℣. I. Dominus regnavit decore. ℣. II. Mirabilis in excelsis Dominus. COM. Exulta filia Sion. PSALM. Lauda Gerusalem. AD REPET. Quonium confortavit.
IN DIE NATALIS DOMINI. AD SANCTUM PETRUM.	VIII KALENDAS JANUARIAS IN DIE NATALIS DOMINI STATIO AD SANCTUM PETRUM. [CAP.] XI.	IN DIE NATALIS DOMINI QUE EST VIII KALENDAS JANUARIAS. STATIO AD SANCTUM PETRUM.
[ANT.] Puer natus est nobis et filius datus est nobis cujus imperium super humerum ejus et vocabitur nomen ejus magni consilii Angelis. PSALM. Cantate Domino quia mirabilia. AD REPET. Notum fecit. RESP. GRAD. Viderunt omnes fines terrɇ salutare Dei nostri jubilate Deo omnis terra. ℣. Notum fecit Dominus salutare suum ante conspectu gentium revelabit justitiam suam.	ANT. (Authenticus Tetrardus.) Puer natus est nobis et filius natus est nobis cujus imperium super humerum ejus et vo[ca]bitur nomen ejus magni consilii Angelus. PSALM. Cantate Domino. II. RESP. GRAD. Viderunt omnes fines terrae salutare Dei nostri jubilate Domino omnis terra. ℣. Notum fecit Dominus salutare suum ante conspectum gentium revelavit justitiam suam.	[ANT.] Puer natus est nobis. PSALM. Cantate Domino. II. AD REPET. Notum fecit Dominus. RESP. GRAD. Viderunt omnes fines terre. ℣. Notum fecit Dominus.

ex. A.12

(1) AM 218

E- go au- tem ad Dó- mi-num ad-spí- ci- am, et ex- péc-ta- bo De- um Sal-va-tó- rem me- um.

(2) AM 215

Prop- ter Si- on non ta- cé- bo, do- nec e-gre-di- á- tur ut splen-dor ius- tus e- ius.

(3) AM 218

Ve- ni Dó-mi- ne, et no-li tar-dá- re: re- lá- xa fa- ci-no-ra ple- bi tu- æ Is- ra- el.

(4) AM 201

Si- on re- no- vá-be- ris, et vi- dé- bis ius-tum tu- um, qui ven-tú-rus es in te.

ex. A.13 GR 32

D ó- mi- ne De- us vir- tú- tum, con-vér- te

nos: et ostén- de fá- ci- em tu- am,

et sal- vi é- ri- mus. ℣. Ex-ci- ta

Dó- mi- ne, pot-én- ti- am tu- am,

et ve- ni, ut sal- vos fá- ci- as nos.

ex. A.14 GR 172

D ó-mi- ne,   ex- áu- di   o-ra- ti- ó-nem

me-   am,   et cla- mor me-   us   ad

te   vé-   ni- at.

℣ 2. Ne a-vér-   tas   fá-ci- em tu-   am   a

me: in qua-cúmque di- e trí-   bu- lor,   in- clí-

na   ad me   aurem tu-   am.

℣ 3. In qua-cúmque di-   e   in-vo-cá- ve- ro te,

ve- ló-   ci- ter   ex-áu- di me.

℣ 4. Qui- a de- fe-cé-   runt sic-ut fu-   mus

di- es me-   i: et ossa me-   a   sic- ut

in fri-xó-   ri- o   con-frí-   xa sunt.

ex. A.14 (cont.)

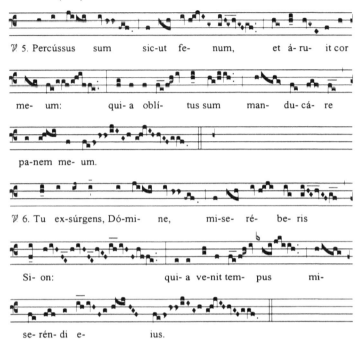

℣ 5. Percússus   sum   sic-ut   fe-   num,   et á- ru-   it cor

me-   um: qui- a   oblí-   tus sum   man-   du- cá-   re

pa-nem me- um.

℣ 6. Tu   ex-súrgens, Dó-mi-   ne,   mi-se-   ré-   be- ris

Si- on: qui- a ve-nit tem-   pus   mi-

se- rén- di e-   ius.

ex. A.15 GR 122

S æ-pe   ex-pu-gna- vé- runt me   a iu- ven-

tú- te me-   a.

𝒱 2. Di-   cat nunc   Is- ra- el: sæ-pe

ex-pu-gna- vé-runt me   a iu- ven- tú- te me-

a.

𝒱 3. Et- e-   nim   non po- tu- é- runt mi- hi:

supra dor-sum me-   um   fabri-ca-vé-   runt pec- ca-

tó-   res.

𝒱 4. Pro- longa- vé-   runt   in- i- qui- tá- tem si- bi:

Dó-mi-nus ius-tus   con- cí- det   cer-

ví- ces pec- ca- tó-   rum.

ex. A.16 GR 186

C anté- mus Dó- mi-no: glo-ri- ó-se e- nim

ho-no- ri- fi- cá- tus est: equum et a-scen- só- rem pro-

ié- cit in ma- re: ad-iú-tor et pro-téctor fac-tus est

mi-hi in sa- lú- tem.

℣ 2. Hic De-us me- us, et ho-no-rá-bo e- um: De-us pa-tris

me- i, et ex-al- tá- bo e- um.

℣ 3. Dó- minus cónte-rens bel- la: Dó- mi- nus no- men

est il- li.

ex. A.17

(1) AM 1145

O - rán- te sancto Cle-mén- te,   appá-ru- it e- i A-gnus

De- i.

(2) AM 1145

N on me- is mé- ri- tis   ad vos me mi- sit Dó-mi-nus,   vestris

co-ró- nis par-tí- ci- pem me fī- e- ri.

(3) AM 1145

V i- di supra mon-tem   A-gnum stan-tem, de sub cu-ius pe- de

fons vi- vus e-má- nat.

(4) AM 1145

D e sub cu- ius pe-de   fons vi-vus e-má- nat: flú-mi- nis ímpe-

tus læ-tí- fi-cat   ci-vi- tá-tem De- i.

ex. A.18

(1) AM 793

L i-bén-ter glo- ri- á- bor in in-fir-mi- tá- ti- bus me- is, ut in

há- bi- tet in me vir-tus Chris- ti.

(2) AM 793

D a- másci, præ-pó- si- tus gen-tis A-ré- tæ re-gis vó- lu- it me

comprehén-de-re: a frá-tri-bus per mu- rum submís-sus sum in spor-

(3) AM 794

T er vir-gis cæ-sus sum, se-mel la- pi- dá- tus sum: ter naufrá- gi-

um pér-tu- li pro Chris- ti nó-mi- ne.

ex. A.19

Cod. Paris, Bibl. Nat. lat. 12050 Gradual of Corbie, late ninth century

ex. A.20

Sacramentary for Essen (Germany), perhaps edited at Corvey
(Neu-Corbie) or at Hildesheim, ninth century

ex. A.21

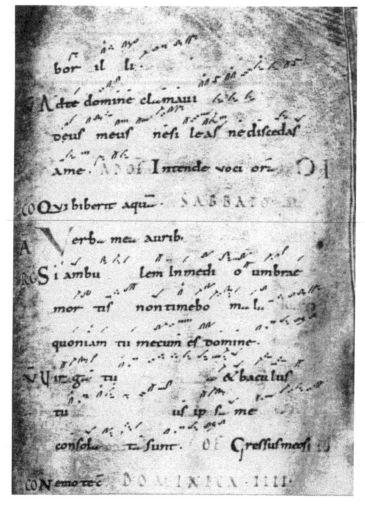

Cod. St. Gallen, Stiftsbibl. 359, Cantatorium, beginning of tenth century

ex. A.22

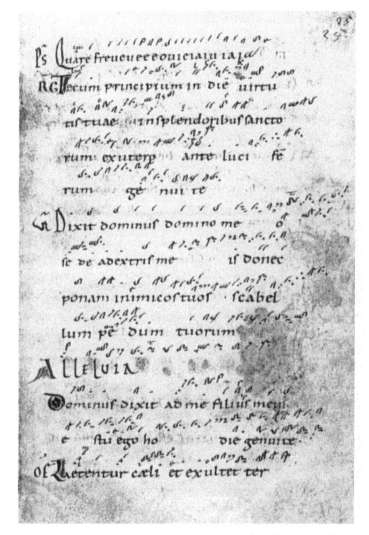

Cod. Einsiedeln, Stiftsbibl. 121, Gradual, end of tenth century, between
964 and 971

ex. A.23

Cod. Laon, Bibl. Municipale 239, Gradual, end of tenth century ca. 930

ex. A.24

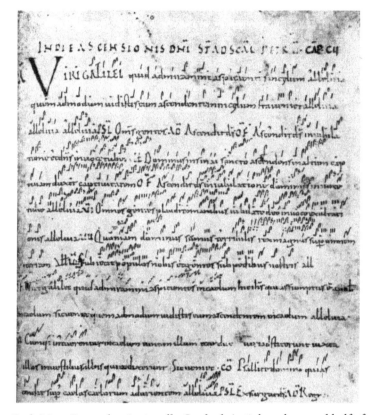

Cod. Mont-Renaud, private coll., Gradual-Antiphonal, second half of
tenth century

ex. A.25

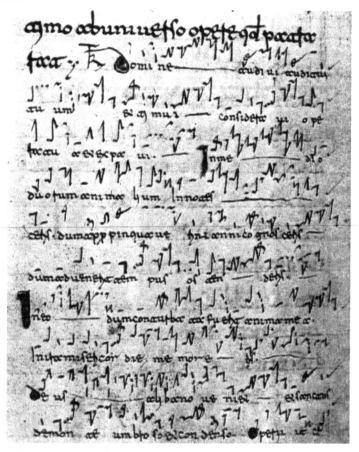

Cod. Benevento, Bibl. Cap. 33, Missal, tenth to eleventh centuries.

ex. A.26

Cod. Benevento, Bibl. Cap. 40, Gradual, beginning of eleventh century

ex. A.27

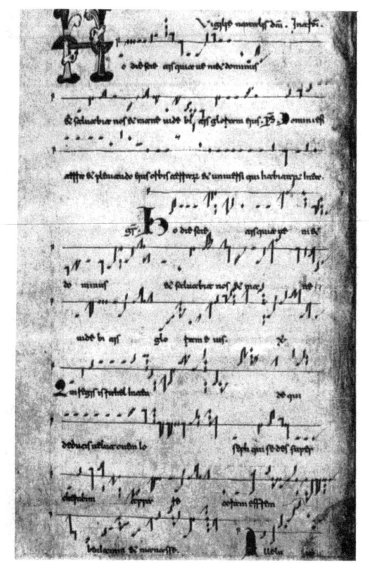

Cod. Benevento, Bibl. Cap. 34, Gradual, eleventh to twelfth centuries

ex. A.28

Cod. Roma, Angelica 123, Gradual of Bologna, beginning of
eleventh century

ex. A.29

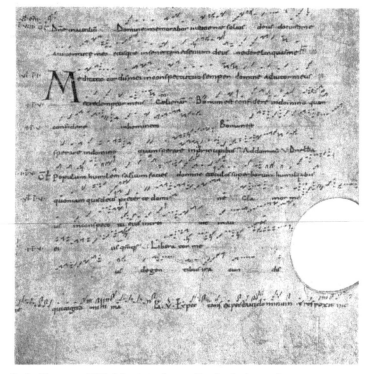

Cod. Chartres, Bibl. Municipale 47, Gradual, eleventh century

ex. A.30

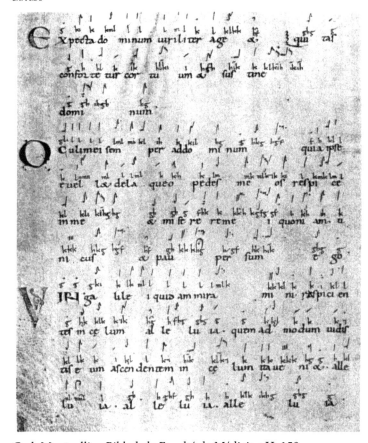

Cod. Montpellier, Bibl. de la Faculté de Médicine H. 159,
Gradual-Tonary, eleventh century

ex. A.31

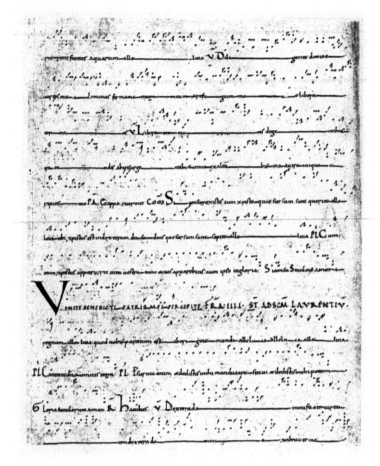

Cod. Paris, Bibl. Nat. laat 776, Gradual of Gaillac (Albi), second half of
eleventh century

ex. A.32

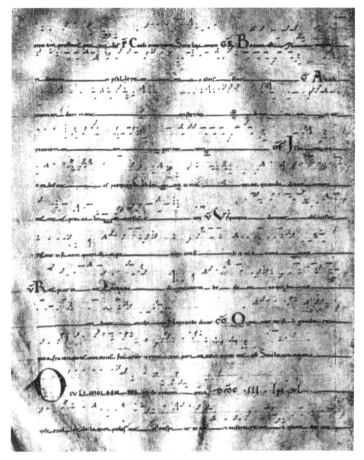

Cod. Paris, Bibl. Nat. lat. 903, Gradual of Saint-Yrieix, eleventh century

ex. A.33

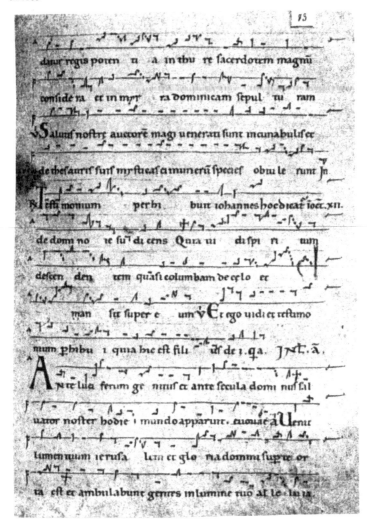

Cod. Lucca, Bibl. Cap. 601, Monastic Antiphonal, twelfth century

ex. A.34

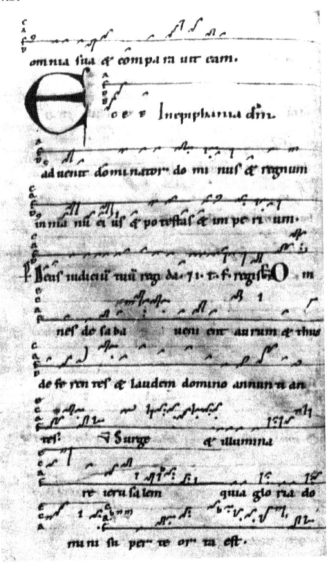

Cod. Graz, Universitätsbibliothek 807, Gradual of Klosterneuburg,
second half of twelfth century

ex. A.35

Cod. Worcester, Bibl. Cath. F 160, Monastic Antiphonary, thirteenth century

ex. A.36

224   HUCBALDI COMMEMORAT. BREVIS

benedictionem a Domino, & misericordiam a Deo.   Quoniam alieni insurrexe-

runt adverfum me, & fortes quæfierunt animam meam, & non propofuerunt.

V. MODUS.

Iuftitiæ Domini rectæ lætificantes corda, præceptum Domini.

VI. MODUS.

Deus Deus meus refpice me, quare me dereliquifti.

QUINTUS TONUS.

Gloria. feculorum amen.   Solvite templum hoc.   Seculorum amen.   Vox

clamantis.   *Pfalmus:*   Confitebor tibi Domine in toto corde meo, quoniam

audifti verba oris mei.   Adorabo ad templum fanctum tuum, & confitebor no-

mini tuo.   Super misericordia tua & veritate tua, quoniam.   In quacumque

die invocavero te exaudi me, multiplicabis.   Confitebor tibi Domine omnes

reges terræ, quoniam.   Quoniam magna eft gloria Domini, quoniam.   Si

ambulabis in medio tribulationis vivificabis me, & fuper iram inimicorum meo-

rum extendes manum tuam, & falvum me fecit.   Domine retribue pro me,

Domine mifericordia tua in feculum, & opera manuum.   Dominus regnavit, exul-

Commemoratio brevis de tonis et Psalmis modulandis of Hucbald, monk of St. Amand, late tenth to early eleventh centuries, p. 224

ex. A.37

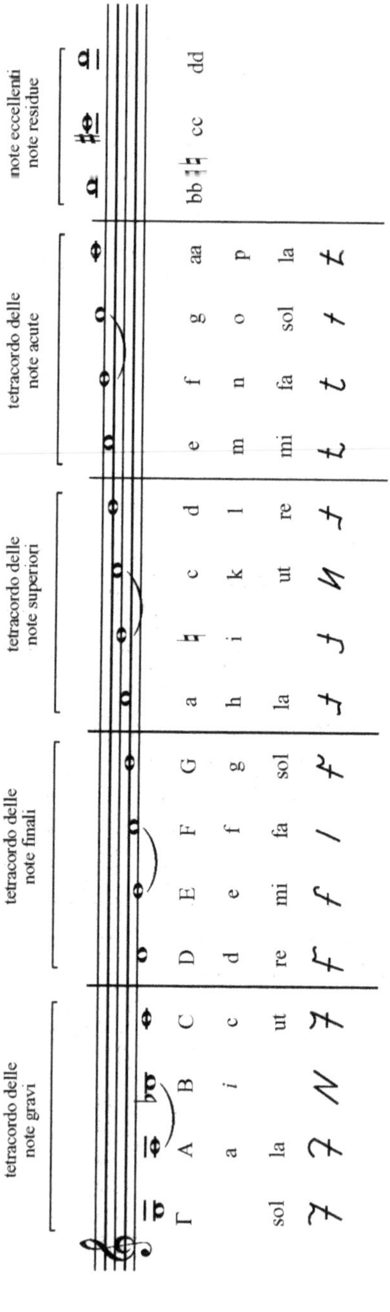
tetracordo delle note gravi
tetracordo delle note finali
tetracordo delle note superiori
tetracordo delle note acute
note eccellenti note residue
Γ A B C D E F G a ♮ c d e f g aa bb ♮ cc dd
a i c d e f g h i k l m n o p
sol la ut re mi fa sol la ut re mi fa sol la

ex. A.38

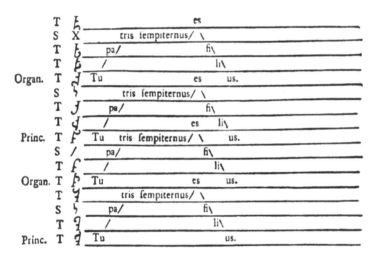

Musica enchiriadis of Hucbald, SE, pp. 158 and 166

ex. A.39

GM 50

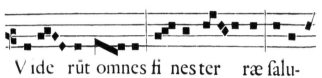

Vide rūt omnes fi nes ter ræ falu-

GR 50

CO. I

V   I-dé- runt omnes *   fi-nes ter- rae   sa-lu-

tare   De i no ftri.

tá-   re   De-   i   no-stri.

ex. A.40

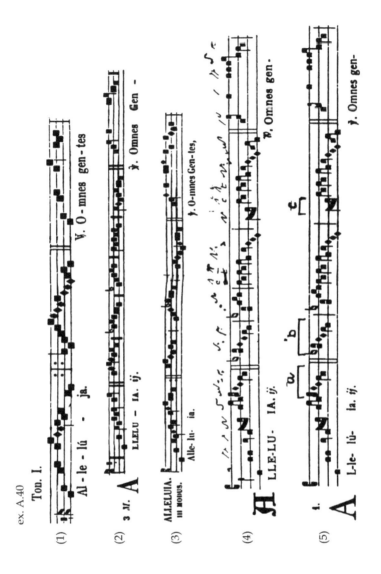

ex. A.40 (cont.)

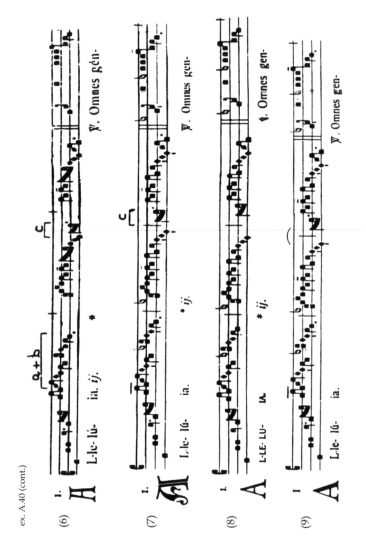

ex. A.41

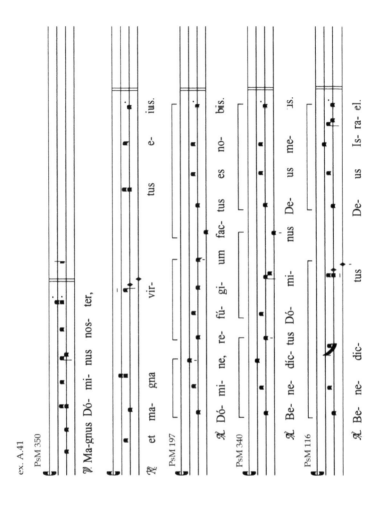

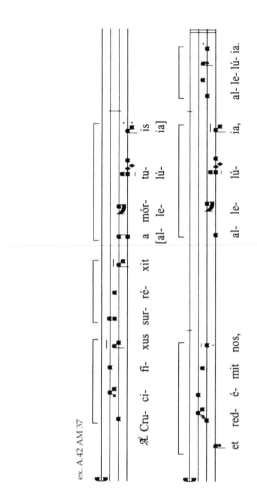

ex. A.42 AM 37

℟. Cru- ci- fi- xus sur- ré- xit a mór- tu- [al- le- lú- is ia]

et red- é- mit nos, al- le- lú- ia, al- le- lú- ia.

ex. A.43

KS 24
Ky- ri- *ee*- léi- son.
KR XVIII
Ky- ri- *ee*- léi- son. Chris- *tee*- léi- son. Ky- ri- *ee*- léi- son.
KR XV
Ky- ri- *ee*- léi- son. Chris- *tee*- léi- son. Ky- ri- *ee*- léi- son.
Ky- ri- *ee*- léi- son. Ky- ri- *ee*- léi- son.
Ky- ri- *ee*- léi- son.

ex. A.44

(1) HISP (ex Prosario Oscensi, sec. XI/XII)

Lau- dá-mus   te.   Be- ne- di- ci- mus   te.   Ad-o- rá-mus   te.   Glo- ri- fi- cá-mus   te.

(2) GREG (GR II*)

Lau- dá-mus   te.   Be- ne- di- ci- mus   te.   Ad-o- rá-mus   te.   Glo- ri- fi- cá-mus   te.

(3) GREG (GR XI)

Lau- dá-mus   te.   Be- ne- di- ci- mus   te.   Ad-o- rá-mus   te.   Glo- ri- fi- cá-mus   te.

(4) MIL (AMM 610)

Lau- dá-mus   te.   Be- ne- di- ci- mus   te.   Ad-o- rá-mus   te.   Glo- ri- fi- cá-mus   te.

ex. A.44 (cont.)

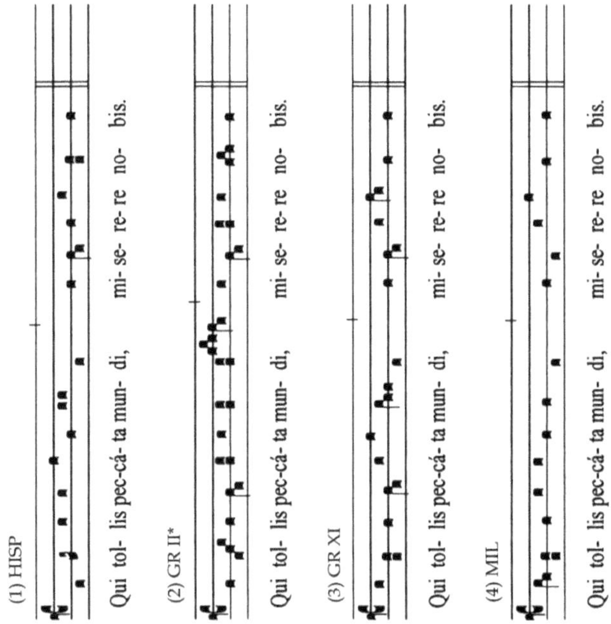

(1) HISP

Qui tol- lis pec-cá- ta mun- di, mi- se- re- re no- bis.

(2) GR II*

Qui tol- lis pec-cá- ta mun- di, mi- se- re- re no- bis.

(3) GR XI

Qui tol- lis pec-cá- ta mun- di, mi- se- re- re no- bis.

(4) MIL

Qui tol- lis pec-cá- ta mun- di, mi- se- re- re no- bis.

ex. A.45

1. Te De- um lau- dá- mus: te Dó- mi- num con- fi- té- mur.

2. Te De- um lau- dá- mus: te Dó- mi- num con- fi- té- mur.

3. Te De- um lau- dá- mus: te Dó- mi- num con- fi- té- mur.

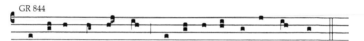

4. Te De- um lau- dá- mus: te Dó- mi- num con- fi- té- mur.

5. Te De- um lau- dá- mus: te Dó- mi- num con- fi- té- mur.

ex. A.45 (cont.)

(1) Te æ- tér-num Pa- trem omnis ter-ra ve- ne- rá- tur.

(2) Te æ- tér-num Pa- trem omnis ter-ra ve- ne- rá- tur.

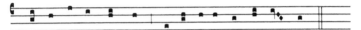

(3) Te æ- tér-num Pa- trem omnis ter-ra ve- ne- rá- tur.

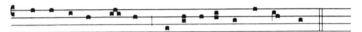

(4) Te æ- tér-num Pa- trem omnis ter-ra ve- ne- rá- tur.

(5) Te æ- tér-num Pa- trem omnis ter-ra ve- ne- rá- tur.

ex. A.45 (cont.)

(1) Sanc-   tus,   San-   ctus,   Sanc-   tus.

(2) Sanc-   tus,   Sanc-   tus,   Sanc-   tus.

(3) Sanc-   tus,   Sanc-   tus,   Sanc-   tus.

(4) Sanc-   tus,   Sanc-   tus,   Sanc-   tus.

(5) Sanc-   tus,   Sanc-   tus,   Sanc-   tus.

ex. A.46

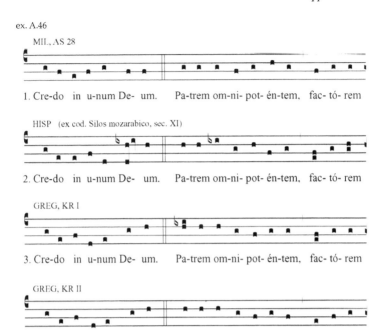

MIL., AS 28

1. Cre-do in u-num De- um.   Pa-trem om-ni- pot- én-tem, fac- tó- rem

HISP (ex cod. Silos mozarabico, sec. XI)

2. Cre-do in u-num De- um.   Pa-trem om-ni- pot- én-tem, fac- tó- rem

GREG, KR I

3. Cre-do in u-num De- um.   Pa-trem om-ni- pot- én-tem, fac- tó- rem

GREG, KR II

4. Cre-do in u-num De- um.   Pa-trem om-ni- pot- én-tem, fac- tó- rem

ex. A.46 (cont.)

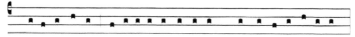

(1) cæ-li   et ter-ræ,   vi- si-bí- li- um ómni- um   et   in-vi- si- bí- li- um.

(2) cæ-li   et ter-ræ,   vi- si-bí- li- um ómni- um   et   in-vi- si- bí- li- um.

(3) cæ-li   et ter-ræ,   vi- si-bí- li- um ómni- um   et   in-vi- si-bí- li-   um.

(4) cæ-li   et ter-ræ,   vi- si-bí- li- um ómni- um   et   in-vi- si- bí- li- um.

GLOSSARY

Accentuation
From the medieval Latin *accentus*. Not to be equated merely with the word accents, this term refers to a harmonious coordination of the different qualities of the syllables of a word and/or phrase.

Ante oblationem
Before the offering of the gifts at Mass.

Antiphonale Monasticum
The liturgical book containing the monastic arrangement of the Office antiphons and other chants used at the Hours (prayers) of the day.

Antiphonale pro diurnis horis
The liturgical book containing the chants for the Hours (of prayer) during the day.

Chant Propers of the Mass (*Proprium Missæ*)
The chants of the Mass whose texts change in relation to the liturgical season, or other liturgical occasions. The propers are of two types: processional chants, and the chants associated with the Mass readings.
  A. **Processional chants**: Introit (entrance), Offertory, Communion.
  B. **Chants of the Readings**: Gradual, Tract, Canticle, *Alleluia*, Sequence.

Codex (codices, plural)
An ancient bound handwritten document.

Cursus, the Monastic *cursus*, the Roman cursus

The chants for the course of each day of the Divine Office as arranged for the monastic communities or for Roman clergy.

Desclée & Socii. S. Sedis Apostolicæ et Sacrorum Rituum Congregationis Typographi

Belgian publishers of some of the first printed editions of Gregorian Chant in the twentieth century.

Dieresis/Syneresis

The phenomenon of *syneresis/dieresis* is commonly found in the melodic genre of the "melody-type" treated earlier in this volume in the introduction at n. 2 (Historical Overview). In chapter 3, the antiphon *Venite adoremus eum*, ex. 3.53 (1), the first two syllables of the word adoremus each receive a monosonic neume. In the second antiphon, *Data est mihi*, at the corresponding point in the melody, the first syllable of om-nis receives a two-note neume. In the comparison of the two antiphons, the first two syllables of ad-o-remus are said to be in dieresis (separated) in relation to the first syllable of om-nis, which is in a relation of *syneresis* (joined).

Epenthesis

A term in phonology that refers to the adding of a sound to a word, as in: film=filum. The *epenthesis* is commonly used in the cadences of the Gregorian Psalm-tones where it is notated as an empty notehead, and where it appears in two forms, anticipated or intercalated.

In nocte Nativitatis Domini ad Matutinum, Missam et Laudes

A liturgical book containing the night of Christmas, including Mass at night, the Offices of Matins and Lauds for the birth of the Lord (Christmas).

Kyriale

Liturgical book containing the chants of the Ordinary of the Mass: *Kyrie, Gloria, Credo, Sanctus*, and *Agnus Dei*.

Liturgical cycles
The liturgical year (since Vatican II) consists of the cycles of Advent, Christmas, Lent, Easter, Ordinary Time, and Sanctoral (Cycle of Saints).

Monody
A type of music with a single melodic line.

"Movable tone"
Term that refers to B-natural or B-flat, both of which are commonly found in the melodies of Gregorian Chant.

Neumatic break
A term used by Dom Eugène Cardine, to describe and interpret the graphic modification of certain neumes in medieval notation, indicating a corresponding modification of its performance.

Ordinarium Missæ
The Chants of the Ordinary of the Mass: see above at Kyriale.

Oxytone, Paroxytone, Proparoxtytone
An **oxytone** is a one-syllable word with a tonic accent (Rex, laus, cor). A word with two syllables that carries the accent on the first syllable is called a **paroxytone**. A word with three syllables with the accent on the first syllable and whose penultimate syllable is considered brief is called a **proparoxtytone.**

Paleography
Paleography is the scientific study of ancient systems of writing with the intention of deciphering and reading them with precision, and determining their historical and geographical origins.

Semiology

Inaugurated by Dom Eugène Cardine, OSB (1905–88), monk of the Abbey of Solesmes, Gregorian semiology is the study of the interpretation of ancient Gregorian neumatic notation.

Semitonal note

SI (B) one half-step (or semi-tone) under DO (C), or MI (E) one half-step (or semi-tone) under FA (F).

"Strong-tone"

Term that refers either to DO (C) or to FA (F), the two pitches that sit directly above the half- steps in the Gregorian modal scale.

Syllable-neume

As in **accent syllable-neume, pre-tonic syllable-neume,** etc. Since every neume is the equivalent of both a single syllable and a specific melodic element (pitch or group of pitches), the terminology "syllable-neume" emphasizes the connection (symbiosis) of word and melody as a fundamental characteristic of the Gregorian melody.

Syllabic articulation

This is the action of passing from one syllable in a word to the next; **verbal articulation** is the action of the passing from one word to the next.

Word-melody

This term defines a melisma, or jubilus, as consisting of a structure analogous to, or similar to, a word, insofar as it resembles a word in its grouping of syllables.